PRAISE FOR
WHEN YOUR WAY ISN'T WORKING

Kyle Idleman, one of my favorite authors, did it again! Are you feeling discouraged or exhausted and don't know why? In *When Your Way Isn't Working*, Kyle offers questions that help his readers understand what is off and the *only* way that works. Kyle reminds us that Jesus is who we need most and helps us find a deeper connection with him.

> **Jonathan Pokluda,** lead pastor of Harris Creek Baptist Church, bestselling author, and host of the *Becoming Something* podcast

In a season of restless discouragement and persistent anxiety, what we desperately need is not a new strategy for greater productivity; it's an invitation to deeper intimacy with the Almighty. Thank you, Kyle, for this beautiful blend of grace and truth!

> **Ben Stuart,** pastor, Passion City Church, Washington, DC, and author of *Single, Dating, Engaged, Married* and *Rest & War*

We go to great lengths to manage our lives and control our emotions. But our coping mechanisms only take us so far. When the stresses of life press in, our well-constructed ideas start to crumble. We react instead of respond; we feel annoyed instead of compassionate; we tend to isolate ourselves instead of engaging with our community. What's the answer? Deepening our connection with Jesus. Kyle Idleman has written a brilliant, honest book about life, Jesus, and how to abide more deeply in him. Jesus is the answer to every question and the solution to every problem. The words on these pages are funny, accessible, and wonderfully insightful. You'll love this book.

> **Susie Larson,** bestselling author, national speaker, and talk radio host

When Your Way Isn't Working is a clarion call to cling to the Vine. Let's be honest, we all need that. It's not necessarily that Kyle Idleman's exegesis is revolutionary; it's that his own transparency is convicting. He's not a megachurch pastor who pontificates but a beleaguered pilgrim who is vexed by his own longing to reconnect with Jesus. I'm in, Kyle.★

★Kyle's footnotes are worth the price of admission. Skipping them is like missing the water cooler gossip at the office Christmas party.

Mark E. Moore, PhD, teaching pastor at Christ's Church of the Valley, Phoenix, Arizona

Kyle Idleman nailed it. This book is going to be foundational for people. This *is* the way to contentment.

Brant Hansen, radio host, author of *Unoffendable* and *The Men We Need*, and advocate for CURE International Children's Hospitals

In John 15, Jesus uses the imagery of a vine and branches to illustrate our need to be intimately connected to Him. In *When Your Way Isn't Working*, my friend Kyle Idleman unpacks this rich section of Scripture and explains how being connected to Jesus gives us purpose, perspective, and freedom.

Jim Daly, president, Focus on the Family

WHEN
YOUR
WAY
ISN'T
WORKING

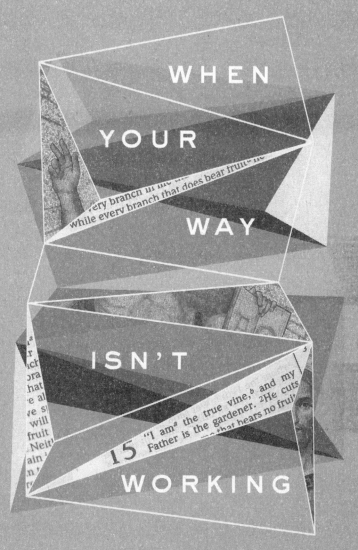

WHEN YOUR WAY ISN'T WORKING

Finding Purpose and Contentment through Deep Connection with Jesus

KYLE IDLEMAN

ZONDERVAN
BOOKS

ZONDERVAN BOOKS

When Your Way Isn't Working
Copyright © 2023 by Kyle Idleman

Requests for information should be addressed to:
Zondervan, *3900 Sparks Dr. SE, Grand Rapids, Michigan 49546*

Zondervan titles may be purchased in bulk for educational, business, fundraising, or sales promotional use. For information, please email SpecialMarkets@Zondervan.com.

ISBN 978-0-310-36398-9 (hardcover)
ISBN 978-0-310-36765-9 (international trade paper edition)
ISBN 978-0-310-36400-9 (audio)
ISBN 978-0-310-36399-6 (ebook)

The author is represented by the literary agent Don Gates @ THE GATES GROUP, www.the-gates-group.com.

Cover design: Faceout Studio
Cover illustrations: Susana Martins, Arcangel; Godong Photo, Adobe Stock; IngridHS, Shutterstock
Interior design: Denise Froehlich

Printed in the United States of America

23 24 25 26 27 LBC 5 4 3 2 1

To my Southeast staff family—
every day I am so thankful
to call each of you partners in the gospel
and that together we get to be Jesus' branches.

CONTENTS

DIAGNOSING DISCONNECTION

Apart from me you can't do anything.

—JESUS

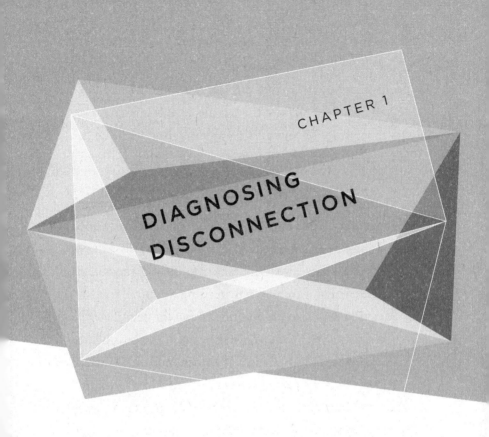

CHAPTER 1

DIAGNOSING DISCONNECTION

I have a friend who is an executive coach. I think you should give him a call."

That suggestion was made to me by a buddy who recognized that my way wasn't working. He worded it more graciously than that. He said something to me like, "You just haven't been yourself lately." My initial response was a combination of being dismissive and defensive, but deep down I knew he was right.

I have never been someone who is easily discouraged. I have rarely felt overly stressed or anxious. I have always been driven and energetic. For most of my life it hasn't been hard to see the potential good and keep a positive perspective. But the last few months had been especially challenging and the people around me could see I was struggling. Meanwhile, I was struggling with the fact that I was struggling, which made my struggling more of a struggle.

The people around me had to *see* it because they weren't hearing about it from me. Not to brag, but I'm really good at not asking people for help. Like super good at it. I'm not saying I can go longer without asking for help than you can, but the fact that you are willingly reading this book is at least an indication that I'm better at not asking for help than you are. I decided a long time ago that I wanted to be a helper, not someone who needed help. It's much more appealing to be a rescuer than the person getting rescued. No one watches *Spider-Man* and fantasizes about being the person hanging helplessly from the balcony hoping to be saved.

I think it's hard for me to ask for help because I don't like to be perceived as weak and I worry that asking for help comes off as whiny. If there is one thing I have a hard time with, it's grown adults, especially men, who whine. I even have a Bible verse for that—Philippians 2:14: "Do everything without grumbling or arguing." I used to keep that verse posted on a wall in both my house and at my office, not so much as a reminder to me but as a warning to everyone else. If you're feeling frustrated, tired, overwhelmed, stressed-out, anxious, discouraged, or depressed, my counsel would have been fairly straightforward: stop feeling that way and do something about it.

That approach worked really well for me—until it didn't. "Don't whine; deal with it" was my way of dealing with discouragement and disappointment, but it was becoming increasingly clear to the people around me that my way wasn't working.

The suggestion of an "executive coach" came at a time when I knew I needed help, even if I wasn't willing to say it out loud. Ironically, I'd later discover I was surrounded by people who loved me and wouldn't charge me money for the help. But it felt safer to pay a stranger, so I set up an appointment. A few minutes into our first Zoom meeting, I was struck by a realization about my "executive coach." I was onto him and blew his cover like it was the end of a Scooby-Doo cartoon. "Wait a second! You're a therapist! You just call yourself an 'executive coach' so people like me will talk to you."

I talked to him about my feelings, the best I knew how. Without meaning to, I was suddenly spewing a bunch of frustrations. I told him I was frustrated with the things happening around me that were out of my control. I confessed to him that while I didn't feel burned-out, I sure felt worn-out. I admitted to him that I felt like all I did was disappoint people. Before I knew what was happening, I started to unload:

> Everyone has an opinion about what I should be doing differently or how I could do it better.
> I can't post anything on social media without somebody taking it personally and getting offended.

My list of things that need to get done feels like a weight that's too heavy, but more plates get added to the bar every day.

The people I care about the most are always getting my leftover energy and time.

I'm in over my head. I don't know what I'm doing, and I think everyone around me is starting to figure that out.

I feel like everyone needs something from me and all I do is let them down.

For the first time in my life, I don't feel very motived or driven. I come home from work and just want to lie on the couch and stare at my phone.

Even though I know God's grace, I feel like I'm letting him down. I don't know why he doesn't pull me out of the game and put someone else in.

I feel discouraged, and I'm discouraged about feeling discouraged because I'm supposed to be the one who encourages people who are discouraged.

When I was finished, I was immediately ashamed. My wife would have been proud of me for being vulnerable, but I was sure I sounded weak and pathetic, probably whiny—although at some point, I definitely started to sound more annoyed. I have this thing I do where instead of vulnerably admitting that things are hard and I need help, I act annoyed. I say annoyed, but some people might say angry, but even angry seems better than whiny. It feels more powerful and less helpless.

My ~~executive coach~~ therapist went on to ask me a series of questions. (It reminded me of going to my primary physician, who would run through a list of questions to determine if I'm healthy.) He asked me about my schedule: "How are you sleeping? Are you keeping a consistent routine?" He asked about my relationships: "What kind of time are you spending with your wife? How connected are you with your kids?" He asked about my friendships: "Do you have authentic friendships? Or do you just have buddies and coworkers?" He asked about who I'm honest with: "When was the last time you asked someone to help you or pray for you?"

I was starting to get defensive. "Umm . . . I'm doing it right now, bro."

And then he asked me about my relationship with Jesus: "How connected do you feel to him and how much time do you spend praying and reading Scripture. Are you talking to Jesus about the things you just unloaded on me?"

I wanted to give honest answers to all these questions. I wanted to tell him my life felt out of control, like I was always under water, straining to break through the surface and get a lungful of air. I wanted to tell him I wasn't sleeping well at night because I couldn't turn off the scrolling list of things in my head that I hadn't gotten done that day. I wanted to tell him I felt lonely and that I hadn't been making time for the people closest to me. I wanted to tell him I hadn't been walking as closely with Jesus as I'd like to and how much I missed Jesus.

I wanted to admit that the way I was living wasn't working,

but I didn't say any of those things. Instead, I began to blame people and circumstances over which I had no control.

After my ~~executive coach~~ therapist had completed his questions and I had listed my answers, he asked me a simple question: *"How would you say that's working for you?"*

I couldn't believe he dropped the "how's that working for ya?" question on me. That's the question I ask other people. I don't do much pastoral counseling, but when I do, I almost always ask, "How's that working for ya?"

> *A wife tries to tell her husband what he needs to do*
> *differently . . . How's that working for ya?*
> *A father has been putting in sixty-hour workweeks and his*
> *teenage son is spiraling . . . How's that working for ya?*
> *A young woman is always on social media and everyone*
> *thinks her life is perfect, but she's struggling with*
> *depression . . . How's that working for ya?*
> *You keep cheering for the Detroit Lions . . . How's that*
> *working for ya?*

I've asked that question of the middle-aged man who has all the toys but still feels empty. I've asked it of the alcoholic who is trying to get over their divorce. I've asked it of the woman who is always put together on the outside but feels like her life is out of control. I've asked it of the pastor who feels like it's their job to make everybody happy. I've asked it of the CEO who is killing it at work but is only vaguely aware of what's happening in the lives of their children.

"How's that working for ya?" is the question I ask people who need to make a change. My ~~executive coach~~ therapist asked it more gently and little less passive-aggressively than I would have, but I've asked the question enough to know it's a rhetorical question. The answer was so obvious that it didn't need to be said out loud. We both knew my way wasn't working.

I will somewhat begrudgingly share more of my situation with you in the pages ahead. But as we set out on our journey together, would you start by asking yourself that same question: *How is your way working for you?*

That question may be too general, so let me get a bit more specific. Take a few minutes to think through your answers to these questions:

- Would the people you're closest to say that when they talk to you, you listen well?
- Is it difficult to fall asleep at night? Do you wake up feeling lethargic?
- How do you spend the first fifteen minutes of your morning?
- What's the last thing you do before going to bed at night?
- What's the last passage of Scripture you read and meditated on?
- On average, how much time do you spend a week doing some kind of hobby?
- Are you constantly dropping the ball on basic responsibilities like paying bills or replying to emails?

- Are you having a difficult time keeping commitments?
- How many unread or unanswered texts do you have right now?
- If you're a parent, can you tell me the names of your child's teachers?
- Have you been more irritable and easily annoyed with people?[1]
- Do you spend more time on social media or more time in prayer?
- When was the last time you asked someone for help?
- Have you experienced some weight gain?
- How many times in the past seven days have you exercised?
- Have you experienced an increase in backaches, headaches, or digestive issues?
- How often do you say you're too busy when asked to do something you want to do?
- How often do you volunteer or find ways to serve every month?
- When was the last time you read a book?[2]
- Do you get irrationally upset when the drive-through line is taking too long?
- Have you become more apathetic to things you once cared deeply about?

---

1. If you're not sure, ask your people. If you get annoyed because they take too long to respond or you don't like what they say, you have your answer.
2. You just started this one, so it doesn't count. Good try though.

- Do you increasingly find yourself wanting to be left alone?
- Do you feel your contributions and efforts are often unnoticed or unappreciated?
- Where do you go or what do you do to escape the stress and pressure you feel?
- On a scale of 1 to 10, how defensive and annoyed have these questions made you?

After my first meeting with my ~~executive coach~~ therapist, I was getting ready to start a new sermon series that would expound on John 14–17. Recorded in these chapters of John are the final words of Jesus to his closest followers before his crucifixion. This passage of Scripture is often referred to as the "Farewell Discourse." Four different discourses of Jesus are identified in the Gospels, but this is the longest and certainly the most personal. Jesus knows he doesn't have much time left on earth—his time with the disciples is coming to an end—so he has some things he wants to make sure to say to them.

If you've ever spent time with someone in the final moments of their lives, you know that the conversations are especially personal and intentional. The disciples don't realize that this is the end of their time with Jesus, but he knows full well what is coming. He knows the uncertainty they will experience in the days ahead. He knows the challenges they'll face and the insecurity they'll feel. He knows how overwhelmed they will feel regarding the mission he will give them. He knows how people will misunderstand them and falsely accuse them. He knows they will soon feel worn-out and weak. And Jesus knows that if his disciples try to do things their way, it won't work.

Doing things their way will create division and cause them to turn on each other. Doing things their way will cause them to feel discouraged with the lack of progress. It will make them feel like quitting because of their own inadequacies. It will leave them feeling overwhelmed by everything that is out of their control. Doing things their way will leave them angry with God and with each other, but especially with themselves.

In the second half of this book, we'll be looking at a number of key verses in the Farewell Discourse. However, I want to highlight one verse—John 15:5—as we begin our journey of discovering what to do when your way isn't working. We will walk through the context of John 15:5 in later chapters, but for now we'll let it stand on its own:

> I am the vine; you are the branches. If you remain in me and I in you, you will bear much fruit; apart from me you can do nothing.

The phrase *can do nothing* captures the exasperation of your way that isn't working. You feel like you've put in the work but you're not getting the results. Despite your good intentions and maybe even your disciplined routines, you're not seeing the gains. There are other ways to translate "can do nothing." You might say, "Nothing seems to be working" or "I can't catch a break" or "The deck's stacked against me" or "What's the point?" or "I've tried everything."

When nothing you do is working, Jesus gives a metaphor to help you know what to focus on, and it all comes down to one word: *connection*. Jesus says he is the vine and we are the branches, and as long as we stay connected with him, we will bear much fruit, but apart from him nothing works the way it should.

The word that keeps showing up as Jesus unpacks this metaphor is *remain*. The English Standard Version translates the Greek word *meno* here as "abide." It shows up eleven times in John 15:1–15. In his final moments, Jesus tells his followers again and again to *stay connected with him*. No matter what happens in the future, no matter how discouraged you become, no matter how disappointed you are, no matter how frustrating the situation is, no matter how tired you feel, no matter what trouble you experience, here's the one thing you must never forget to do: *stay connected*.

When your way isn't working, check your connection with the Vine. You are the branch, and the branch's most important job is to stay connected with the Vine.

A Metaphor and a Mantra

Jesus loved to use metaphors and word pictures to help people get their arms around significant and foundational truths. We see all kinds of examples in Scripture. When

Jesus wants his followers to understand how to live in the world, he tells them to be "the salt of the earth" and "the light of the world," like a "town built on a hill" that "cannot be hidden" (Matthew 5:13–14). Jesus reveals himself as the giver of "living water"—the one who is "the bread of life" and "the good shepherd" (John 4:10; 6:35; 10:14). To help us better understand the nature and function of the church, the Bible uses images such as Christ's bride (Ephesians 5:22–23; Revelation 19:7), "God's household" (1 Timothy 3:15), and the body of Christ (1 Corinthians 12:14; Ephesians 4:15–16).

Not only is a metaphor memorable; it can take a complex idea and connect it to a familiar picture so that the listener continues to discover and apply deeper meanings.

While Scripture contains dozens of metaphors, only a handful can be called "controlling metaphors"—which, in literature, are metaphors extended throughout the entire literary piece. Think of a controlling metaphor as the hub of a wheel, with all the spokes connected to that hub.[3] The controlling metaphor anchors[4] the concept and conversation.

I know you may be thinking, *Thanks for the recap of middle school English but let's move on.* But don't skip over this. There is incredible power in identifying a controlling metaphor for your life. These metaphors give us common language, clear direction, and a firm foundation.

Some friends of ours who have been married nearly

---

3. Bonus points if you recognized that I used a metaphor as a way to explain a metaphor.
4. Yep, that's another one.

twenty years were ready to call it quits. They went to a marriage counselor, who asked each of them separately for their side of the story and took careful notes and then brought them back together. At the end of the first session, the counselor said, "Before you go, I want to read several different words the two of you used to describe how you relate to each other." He proceeded to read a sampling of their quotes:

She is constantly *attacking*.

He is always *defending* himself.

I make one mistake, and she's ready to *go to war*.

We've tried a *cease-fire* but it never lasts.

I feel like she's always *locked and loaded* and waiting for me to mess up.

Yeah, I *attacked* first, but it was a *preemptive strike* because I knew what was coming.

And the counselor told our friends that according to his count, they had used the word *fight* or some variation of it twenty-seven times.

He explained to them that the controlling metaphor for their marriage at that point was a war. Without intending to, battle imagery was the word picture they used again and again to describe their marriage relationship. Attack. Conflict. Fight. Defend. Oppose. Struggle. This was the lens through which they viewed their marriage. If war were to continue to be their controlling metaphor, they'd keep responding as enemy combatants.

The marriage counselor explained that our friends needed a new controlling metaphor for their marriage. As the counselor listened to their story, he had jotted in his notes that early in their marriage, they would often go dancing. In fact, they had even taken ballroom dancing lessons together.[5] The marriage counselor suggested that they work at switching marriage metaphors. Instead of thinking of marriage as a *fight*, they needed to think of marriage as a *dance*.

When my buddy shared this solution with me, my first thought was, *That sounds nice, but I'm not sure the metaphor switch is gonna work.* He went on to explain that they were, in fact, learning to dance together. I asked him to unpack that statement a bit more. "Well, we realized pretty quickly," he said, "that our problem seemed to be focused on who should take the lead when it came to different decisions. We were both trying to take the lead all the time, and that wasn't working. So now when I start to feel defensive, I'll say to her, 'I thought I was taking the lead, but I feel like you're stepping on my toes.' And lately we've been talking about how we need to find a rhythm for our relationship that allows us to move together."

A controlling metaphor of *dance* instead of *war* gave them new language, brought some clarity and purpose to their marriage, and opened new pathways for evaluating their

---

5. Something I didn't know about my friend at the time but would certainly make fun of him for.

roles and responsibilities. Sometime later I had a conversation with their counselor, who told me the book *Metaphors We Live By* had changed the way he carried out his therapy.[6] He explained that by guiding people toward finding new controlling metaphors for their struggles, he is able to help them gain a new perspective.

Chances are, if you've heard about controlling metaphors, it was from a literature teacher who talked about the use of extended metaphors in poetry. An example can be found in Emily Dickinson's "Hope Is the Thing with Feathers." For people who are metaphor skeptics, she is gracious enough to give the metaphor away in the first line. Take a moment to read the opening stanza:

> Hope is the thing with feathers
> That perches in the soul,
> And sings the tune without the words
> And never stops at all.[7]

Did you just whip through that? Don't do that to Emily. You can do that to me, but she deserves better. Go back and read it again. Slowly.

The image of hope as feathers that never stop singing is a powerful image. I read of one man whose daughter had become gravely ill. His discouragement was giving way to

---

6. George Lakoff and Mark Johnson, *Metaphors We Live By* (1980; repr., Chicago: University of Chicago Press, 2003).
7. Emily Dickinson, "Hope Is the Thing with Feathers." Public domain.

despair. Someone shared that poem with him and told him not to give up hope. One day while out walking, he saw some feathers in the grass. He picked them up and put them in his pocket as a reminder that hope will never stop singing. Having someone tell him, "Be hopeful," might have been helpful, but the metaphor gave him something to take with him on the hard journey ahead. It gave him a different lens, changing the way he saw his circumstances.

That's what Jesus did for his disciples in his conversation recorded in John 15. He wants to give them something to hold on to when life is hard and nothing seems to be working. So in the cool of the evening as they walked along the streets outside of Jerusalem, he pointed to the vines and branches along the side of the road and said, "I am the vine; you are the branches."

For many years, sitting on my desk in my office was a grapevine. The vine came up from a large vase filled with dirt, and the connected branches sprawled across my desk as a reminder that my primary job description—the singular best practice for me as a husband, father, friend, and pastor—is to be the branch. There are a number of things I can get wrong as long as I get that right. And it doesn't matter what else I get right if I end up getting that wrong.

Language like *remaining*, *abiding*, and *staying connected* doesn't seem overly helpful. My preference is to have a list of actions steps and boxes to check. When my way isn't working, I want a to-do list. I want to be able to take control. I want to be able to put in the work so I can fix what's broken.

Staying connected seems too passive. However, I'm learning that the personal practices that lead to connection require intentionality and work. Connection doesn't just happen.

When your way isn't working and you're not sure what to do, be the branch. If you stay connected with Jesus, you'll bear much fruit, but apart from him you can't do anything.

CHAPTER 2

THE DISCONNECTION DASHBOARD

My wife has made a concerted effort to help me better identify whatever emotion I might be feeling in a particular moment. Ironically, she never asked me how I *felt* about better understanding my feelings. She likely didn't ask because she knew I would respond with, "Fine," which tends to be my go-to answer when trying to describe how I feel. And not to be defensive, but I'm sure I'm not the only person of my gender who uses the word *fine* as an umbrella term for a plethora of unknown and unrecognized emotions. My spectrum of emotions ranges between "fine," "good," and "meh."

To help me better identify my emotions, my wife has a tool she uses that she calls the *Wheel of Emotions*,[1] or as I sometimes call it, the *Wheel of Feel*.

For a period of time, the Wheel of Emotions hung on our refrigerator as a way to help us navigate our feelings as we were raising three teenage daughters. The wheel gives dozens of emotions to choose from. So instead of just saying *angry*, the wheel can help you decide if you actually feel more *withdrawn* or *disrespected*. The idea is that if you can identify the emotion you're feeling at a particular moment, you can better understand what is causing you to feel that way and the direction those feelings will inevitably take you and the people around you.

The word *emotions* comes from the Latin word *emovere*, defined in its simplest terms as "to move." Think of it this way: something moves us *to* an emotion, and an emotion is moving us *to* something. Where we've come from and where we're going in life are significantly determined by our emotions. This is true even if you don't want it to be.

Over the years, here's what I've discovered personally and as a pastor: some common emotions tend to show up when our way isn't working. When we're not living our lives deeply connected with Jesus, certain emotions begin to surface.

Let's go back to our controlling metaphor in John 15:5,

---

1. To help yourself feel more positive about the Wheel of Emotions, I've found that it's best to say it with the excitement and cadence used in the introduction to *The Wheel of Fortune*.

where Jesus tells his disciples, "I am the vine; you are the branches." When I'm doing things *my* way, I've stopped being the branch and am trying to be the vine. I'm trying to live my life out of my own strength and wisdom. I'm trying to bear fruit through my own efforts and desires. Instead of connecting with Jesus and finding what I need in him, I'm trying to find it in myself. As we'll see later, this approach will inevitably stop working, and when it does, some predictable emotions will form.

In an effort to better diagnose the disconnection problem, I've identified some of these emotions in the upcoming chapters. We'll look at examples of people in the Old Testament who experienced some of these emotions—when they kept trying to do things their way. It's not surprising that the Old Testament offers many examples because all of the stories unfolded before Jesus came and made a way for us to be deeply connected with the Vine. In fact, one of the Old Testament's primary purposes was to reveal our need for that connection and to make it clear that without that connection our way would never work.

I should point out that the list of emotions isn't exhaustive, so please consult the Wheel of Emotions for more specific and personal emotions. In addition to the examples from Scripture, I've personally experienced and pastorally seen that this particular combination of emotions often shows up when we live an unabiding life. Think of these emotions as symptoms that point to a diagnosis that our way isn't working.

Gone Fishing

You know who probably could have benefited from the Wheel of Emotions hanging on his refrigerator? Peter. When we meet Peter, he is making a living as a fisherman. And not to stereotype fishermen, but my guess is they might not always be in touch with their feelings. Peter doesn't tell us how he's feeling when his way isn't working, but it's not hard to pick up on some of the emotions lurking under the surface.

In Luke 5, Peter hasn't yet been called to become one of the twelve disciples, but he has been around Jesus enough to know he was an incredible teacher. Peter and his crew pull their two boats up onto the shore and are washing their nets after spending the night fishing on the Sea of Galilee. They are exhausted and ready go home and crash, but Jesus has other plans.

Luke 5:3 tells us that Jesus got into one of the boats. It doesn't appear that Jesus asked. He just climbs into the boat belonging to Peter. I don't think Jesus is being presumptuous here because, after all, Jesus had healed Peter's mother-in-law. So Peter owes him one.[2] Jesus has Peter take him out in the boat so he can teach from there. The natural acoustics of the water would allow the large crowd on the shore to hear him. Verse 4 tells us that when Jesus finishes his address to the crowd, he says to Peter, "Put out into deep water, and let down the nets for a catch."

---

2. Depending on how Peter felt about his mother-in-law.

Peter, a professional fisherman, has been out fishing all night, and now Jesus tells him to go back out and try again. Peter must have been thinking, *Hey, Jesus, I'll leave the teaching to you; you leave the fishing to me. How 'bout you stay in your lane?* What he actually says to Jesus is this: "Master, we've worked hard all night and haven't caught anything" (Luke 5:5).

This is a fishing story, and we associate fishing with a hobby, something we do for fun. But it's a different story for Peter. Fishing isn't something he does just to pass the time; it's what he does to make a living.

When Peter tells Jesus they had worked all night and have nothing to show for it, I wonder how he said it. Maybe he said it quietly, a little embarrassed because fishermen measure their success on their ability to catch fish. After he tells Jesus that despite all of their hard work, they still hadn't caught anything, I wonder if he paused for effect. Maybe a heavy sigh of annoyance. Maybe he took a deep breath in frustration. Or—my personal favorite—maybe he gave a sarcastic "you've gotta be kidding me" chuckle. If my wife would have been on the boat, this is when she would have pulled out the Wheel of Emotions and asked Peter to use his "feeling words."

Peter lets Jesus know he has already tried. He has worked hard and has nothing to show for it. He says they hadn't caught *anything*. Peter acknowledges that his way isn't working, but it's not because of a lack of effort.

My guess is that you've experienced this dynamic in your life. Maybe you're experiencing it now. You've put the work in, expecting to produce a certain result. Yet in spite of all your efforts, you don't have much to show for it.

You've tried hard to turn things around as a parent. You've made an effort to be more consistent with your child. You've been intentional about communicating your expectations. You've worked at responding rather than reacting. But you don't have much to show for it.

You've put in long hours at work. You've taken initiative and made the extra effort. You've asked your boss what you can to do improve, and you've implemented the suggestions. But every time an opportunity arises for a promotion, you get passed over.

You've tried to reconnect with your sibling. From your perspective, you're the only one who's trying. But the more work you put into it, the more indifferent they seem.

You've worked hard on your marriage. You've read books, listened to podcasts, attended conferences. You've even gone to see a counselor. You've trying to learn your spouse's Wheel of Emotions. Despite your best efforts, nothing seems to change. In fact, things seem worse.

When we've put in the work, we have certain expectations of what will be produced. My wife is an avid reader.[3] She goes through books quickly, but I usually keep up with what she's reading because there's always a different book on her nightstand next to the bed.

The other night as I got into bed, I noticed a new book

---

3. Although not always my books. Babe, if you read this footnote, text me "Lulu" and get a free pair of Lululemon leggings.

sitting out, and it was titled *Have a New Husband by Friday.*[4] My first thought was that this was some passive-aggressive way of telling me I'd better make some changes. Then all kinds of questions started coming to mind. First, what does *new* mean? Does "have a new husband by Friday" mean new as in "new and improved" or new as in "brand-new"? Because there's a big difference.

Second, what Friday are we talking about? This Friday? I saw this book on the nightstand on Wednesday night, which didn't give me a lot of time. I began to hope it was a Friday in the distant future. Friday of May 7, 2032, feels like a date I could work toward. But if she's hoping for *this* Friday, she's going to be a little disappointed when she "pulls in the nets."

I'm sure she loved the title of that book because it promised results. We want to know that if we put in the effort, we'll have something to show for it. But when you pull in the nets and don't see *anything*, how does that make you feel? How's that working for ya?

And my wife would tell you that "meh" isn't an acceptable answer.

Four Feelings of Futility

In the next few chapters, I want to identify four primary emotions that show up when your way isn't working. I

---

4. Kevin Leman, *Have a New Husband by Friday: How to Change His Attitude, Behavior, and Communication in Five Days* (Grand Rapids: Revell, 2009).

understand you might feel this combination of emotions to some degree on any given day. I think that's because on any given day we experience the reality of our way not working. You may experience this cocktail of emotions in some seemingly insignificant way, like . . . oh, I don't know . . . trying a do-it-yourself repair on a leaky toilet that won't stop leaking no matter how many parts you replace.

Whether the stakes are relatively low or undeniably high, you can expect these four emotions to show up. Sometimes these emotions are progressive in nature, one emotion leading to another. And sometimes they like to team up and come all at once. But when you are consistently experiencing some combination of these emotions, you can almost conclude that your way isn't working.

Imagine a car's dashboard with a number of gauges that indicate the health of your vehicle and alert you to what may need attention. As we look at these emotions, think of a dashboard and each emotion as a different gauge that indicates how disconnected we might be.

I'll list and define the four emotions here and then take time to unpack them in the upcoming chapters.

1. Discouragement

Definition: A loss of confidence and enthusiasm.

"When nothing changed between the mother and her teenage daughter, she struggled to not give in to discouragement."

2. Fatigue

Definition: Extreme physical and mental tiredness that comes from a prolonged period of concentrated exertion.

"He started off strong, but his pace wasn't sustainable and so fatigue set in."

3. Frustration

Definition: The feeling of being upset or annoyed, especially because of an inability to change or achieve something.

"When she didn't respond the way he expected her to, he slammed the door in frustration."

4. Anxiety

Definition: The feeling of worry or unease, typically when facing an imminent event or uncertain outcome you have no control over.

"The five-year plan for his new business was turned upside down by an unexpected pandemic and left him feeling overwhelmed with anxiety."

On the dashboard of your car, there are likely a few gauges you pay close attention to, a few you're vaguely aware of, and perhaps even a few you know nothing about. You might continually check the gas gauge, but you'll ignore the battery gauge until your car doesn't start. In other words, we don't focus on the gauges until we know there's a problem. But this inattention isn't an especially effective way to drive our cars.

I remember the day when our youngest daughter, who was nineteen at the time, called me on FaceTime while on the road in San Diego, where she was living at the time. When I answered, all I could see was smoke and all I could hear was the noise of traffic as cars flew by on the California expressway. She seemed to be taking everything in stride, calmly saying to me, "Hey, Dad, I think something is wrong with my car."

She had popped the hood and smoke was pouring out of it. I explained that her car was overheating and that she needed to turn off the engine and call AAA. A few minutes later, she FaceTimed me back, and I described in more detail what had happened to her car. I had her get back into the car and flip the camera around to face the dashboard. Pointing out the temperature gauge, I explained that its purpose was to indicate whether her engine is close to overheating. I asked if she had noticed if her vehicle had been running hot, and she informed me that she never checked that gauge because she never knew it existed.

The manufacturer put that gauge on the dashboard to warn drivers of a problem. If a driver doesn't look at the dashboard and pay attention to the blinking lights, then the car might be okay—for a while. But eventually it will stop working.

As we consider these four emotions, we may be inclined to overlook them. And that may work for a while. But if we keep ignoring these emotions, sooner or later, we can expect to find ourselves pulled over on the side of the road, with smoke pouring out of our engine.

Let Down the Nets

Before exploring some of the emotions that come when we're not living our best "branch life," we must consider Peter's response to Jesus. Peter's way isn't working and Jesus tells Peter he wants him to do the same thing he's been doing—except this time he wants Peter to do it with Jesus in the boat.

Peter has been fishing all night and hasn't caught anything. When he expresses to Jesus the reality of his situation, he is probably hoping for some encouragement and understanding. When we work hard but aren't getting the desired results, we want the people around us to say things like, "I'll give you an A for effort" or "You gave it your best" or "Maybe things will work out next time" or "There's nothing more you could have done." We want to believe that those things are true.

Peter waits in the silence for Jesus to change his mind about going back out and casting his nets again. But when that doesn't happen, Peter gives the only right response when you discover your way isn't working. Peter says, "But because you say so, I will let down the nets" (Luke 5:5).

Because you say so . . .

As you read through this book, these are the four words I want you to remember. Considering some of the emotions that show up when our way isn't working, I want us to keep in mind that the only right response is, "Because you say so." Remember that emotions are always trying to *move* us somewhere, but Peter's response to Jesus is what moves him more than the way he's feeling in the moment.

Peter didn't feel like doing what Jesus told him to do. He didn't think that what Jesus asked of him would change his situation or produce anything different. What Jesus requested didn't make any sense. Peter was using the same boat and nets, and he was fishing on the same lake. If anything, the conditions for fishing were worse. Jesus tells Peter to go back out into the deep water in the heat of the morning. None of the fishing books would tell you these are best practices.[5] But Peter's response is, "because you say so . . ."

It doesn't make sense to me, but . . . because you say so.

I've tried again and again, but . . . because you say so.

People will think I don't know what I'm doing, but . . . because you say so.

I'm tired and worn-out, but . . . because you say so.

I really don't think this is going to work, but . . . because you say so.

I don't feel like it, but . . . because you say so.

Saying "because you say so" is difficult, especially when it's different from what you want to do or what you think will work. It requires something none of us do very naturally. It requires humble submission.

Humble Submission

A journey to deep connection with Jesus begins with humble submission. It requires an acknowledgment that your way

---

5. At least I don't think so. I've never read a fishing book.

isn't working. Admitting this to yourself is hard enough. Try it. Read this out loud: **My way isn't working.**

If your way was working, would you regularly feel so exhausted and anxious? Would you still be struggling with your addiction? Would you still need to have a drink before going to bed? Would you still feel compelled to look at porn when you feel stressed? Would you still head online and shop when you start to feel overwhelmed?

If your way was working, would you still experience the same turmoil in your relationships? Would you still be losing your temper with your spouse? Would you still have some old friends who no longer talk to you?

If your way was working, would you still be struggling with bitterness and resentment? Would you still feel overwhelmed by fear and anxiety? Would you still be discouraged and ready to quit?

Honestly look around and ask yourself, *If my way was going to work, wouldn't it have worked by now?*

Our journey through the four emotions will require a self-awareness that is impossible without humility. Will we be humble enough to acknowledge that it may be time for a different way? Connection begins when we recognize the reality and the consequences of our disconnection and are willing to do something to change.

Peter doesn't get a reason or an explanation for Jesus' request. He gets no guarantees. That's how most of us want the story to go. In essence, Jesus ends up saying to Peter, "Hey, buddy, I know you're tired. I know you've been working all night. I know you guys are exhausted. I get it—you just cleaned your nets and put them away. I know you don't want to do what I'm going to ask you do. But if you'll take me out with you and fish in the deep water, here's what I'll do for you: I'm going to cause your boats to overflow with fish. Your nets will break because there are so many fish. If you humble yourself and submit to me, here's how I will bless you."

In John 15, Jesus promises us that apart from him we can't do anything, but if we are the branches and stay connected with him as the Vine, we will bear much fruit. I don't know exactly what that looks like or what kind of production you can expect. There are no specific guarantees given, but for Peter the difference between staying up all night without catching anything and then going back out and trying it again is that this time *Jesus is in his boat.* Peter was about to have a front-row seat to discover that, more than his efforts and expertise, it was his connection with Jesus that would lead to production.

Let me repeat that: it's connection that leads to production.

Peter may have thought Jesus didn't know anything about fishing, but he was still willing to humbly submit to him. And here's what Peter learns: Jesus knows everything about everything. It turns out that Jesus has some kind of a built-in fish-finder. Peter just needed to stay connected with Jesus by humbly submitting to him.

It turns out that in any area of your life that doesn't seem to be working, Jesus knows more than you think. He knows more about your job than you do. He knows more about your spouse than you do. He knows more about your children than you do. He knows more about your body than you do. He knows more about your finances than you do. He knows more about you than you do. So as you restart your journey with Jesus, the only way is to commit to humble submission. *That's* where connection begins.

Acknowledging some of the emotions that stem from a disconnected life is hard and humbling, but it's necessary if we're going to experience the fruitful life that comes from a deep connection with Jesus.

In Luke 5, Peter humbles himself and goes back out on the water, but this time Jesus is with him. Peter casts his nets again, and this time there are more fish in the nets than his boat can handle. Verse 8 tells us, "When Simon Peter saw this, he fell at Jesus' knees and said, 'Go away from me, Lord; I am a sinful man!'"

Picture the scene. Peter falls on his knees at the feet of Jesus in the boat. What is he surrounded by? Flopping all around him is evidence that Jesus can do what he can't do. Without connection with Jesus, he can't do anything. But connected with him, he can bear much fruit.

Peter's response to all of this is to repent. Repentance is a humble acknowledgment that our way isn't working and we're ready to go in a different direction.

One of the most encouraging themes of this story—a theme we see throughout Scripture—is that because of Jesus, things don't have to stay the same. The way things are doesn't have to be the way things stay. This time doesn't have to be like the last time.

In the chapters ahead, we'll look at a few examples of Old Testament people and see some of the emotions they experienced when their way wasn't working. Remember that the one thing all of them have in common was that they lived in the BC era. They were trying to make life work without a deep connection with Jesus. Each of their stories is recorded to help us understand that life simply doesn't work when the branch isn't connected with the Vine. The law approach of the Old Testament emphasized working harder and producing more, but the law ultimately showed that trying to do things our way is insufficient. In the Old Testament, the people of God are sometimes referred to as "a vine" (Psalm 80:8), but in the New Testament, Jesus comes to be "the true vine" (John 15:1).

As we study these examples I invite you to take an honest look at the dashboard of your life. Check each gauge to see if there is any disconnection that needs to be addressed.

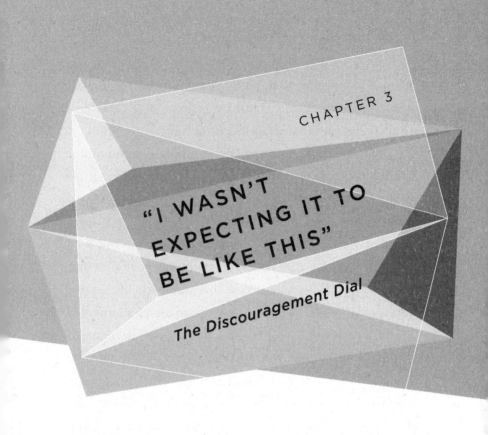

CHAPTER 3

"I WASN'T EXPECTING IT TO BE LIKE THIS"

The Discouragement Dial

Throughout the 1980s and '90s, Bantam released a series of books marketed to kids in elementary and middle school. The series became extremely popular, selling more than 250 million copies. Maybe you remember the series. It was called *Choose Your Own Adventure*.

I was among the gaggle of ten-year-olds anxious for each new release because it wasn't like a normal book. In these books, the reader had options. At different points in the story, the reader could choose a different direction in the plot. The outcome of the story was determined not by the author but by whatever option the reader chose. On the one hand, if you wanted the sheriff to get sucked into the space portal, turn to page 73. On the other hand, turn to page 96 for a way to have the aliens create an alliance with the stagecoach robbers.

The thought that we can choose our own adventure is incredibly appealing. Anytime our way isn't working, no problem. Just stop reading, flip to a different page, and try again. If the ending wasn't what we were hoping for, there are other endings to choose from. Imagine if we had such power in real life. Any time our discouragement dial gets turned up, just choose a different adventure—preferably one where you can avoid adversity and dodge disappointment.

An attempt or two has been made over the years to introduce the "choose your own adventure" genre into the adult market, though without much success. I suspect the reason is that we only have to get a few chapters into this life before we begin to realize how little control we actually have over what happens around us. We start off thinking our stories will unfold a certain way, but they never quite go how we planned. That's when we begin to feel discouraged.

Discouragement sets in when what we experience is different from what we expected.

It's that feeling you get when you step on the scale and the number hasn't changed, even though you've been trying to be more disciplined in your eating and get to the gym more often.

It's that feeling you get when you've prayed the same prayer for months, maybe even years, but God seems silent.

It's that feeling you get when you've been romantically

interested in someone for a while and you finally work up the courage to put yourself out there, only to be told, "You're such a great friend."

It's that feeling you get when you've worked long hours and done your best and then someone else gets the promotion.

It's that feeling you get when you go the extra mile in preparing dinner and no one notices or expresses appreciation.

It's that feeling you get when another pregnancy test is negative.

It's that feeling you get when you know you've done the best you can do, but it isn't good enough.

You know the feeling. You study, but don't get the grade. You practice, but never get in the game. You feel like the interview went well, but they never call back. You apply at the college, but you aren't accepted. You walk out to the mailbox, and you find another letter from a collection agency.

The word is *discouragement*—the loss of hope, confidence, and/or courage. You were feeling hopeful, but then something happened and now you're less hopeful. You had courage and confidence, but things didn't go as planned and now you're not so sure. Discouragement is not an object. It's not something you can see or touch. It doesn't have weight or mass, but that doesn't stop it from holding you back and weighing you down.

The story of Hannah provides an Old Testament case study of someone who felt discouraged. Hannah's way wasn't working, or to put it another way, things weren't working out her way.

We read about Hannah in the book of 1 Samuel. When we meet her, she is already discouraged; in fact, she had been discouraged for a long time. Hannah was married to a man named Elkanah. First Samuel 1:2 tells us "he had two wives; one was called Hannah and the other Peninnah. Peninnah had children, but Hannah had none." Hannah was discouraged because she hadn't been able to conceive.

Uncontrollable Circumstances

It's one thing to deal with disappointment and know you have the power to turn things around. It may not be easy, but you can go back to school or see a marriage counselor or start going to the gym. But your discouragement dial really gets turned up when you don't have any control over the situation. Karen couldn't do anything about the cancer. Mark couldn't force his wife to feel differently. Heather couldn't go back and undo the decision she made in college. And Hannah couldn't do anything about her infertility.

When things aren't going your way, discouragement often compounds the problem.

If you've struggled with infertility, you know how discouraging it can be. In one study, 63 percent of women who experienced both infertility and divorce rated their infertility as more emotionally painful. A counselor friend of mine explained that when a person has a chronic disease or terminal illness, they get support from those around them, but when a couple struggles with infertility, most people around them are not aware of the pain. When your way isn't working and you've decided to keep it to yourself, it turns up your discouragement dial even more.

I'd never minimize the level of disappointment that infertility causes people today, and in Hannah's context, infertility would have been even more discouraging. Having a child was thought of as her primary purpose as a woman and most important contribution as a wife. Society would not have felt compassion for her; rather, a woman who couldn't have children was looked down on—even considered cursed by God.

When life isn't working the way you hoped it would, discouragement sets in and you almost immediately begin blaming God. Discouragement will try to convince you that what you're dealing with is God's fault and that you can only conclude he is against you.

DIY Discouragement

Hannah is married to Elkanah, but Elkanah has a second wife. It's likely that Elkanah had married Hannah first and then, because she was not able to have children, he decided to marry Peninnah. This is one example of polygamy in Scripture—but never confuse the examples as an endorsement. Every instance of polygamy in the Bible seemed to bring nothing but problems. Polygamy is *never* supported in

Scripture. Instead, every example of polygamy serves as a warning: this is a horrible idea, and it was never what God wanted.

I'm sure Elkanah was discouraged when Hannah couldn't bear children. Things weren't going Elkanah's way either, so he decided to take things into his own hands and marry a second wife. At this point, he wasn't just doing things his way; he was doing things the anti-God way. Dealing with discouragement by trying to fix things, even though our efforts mean disobeying God's way, always leads to greater discouragement. Elkanah's DIY approach led to disobedience, which seemed to turn down the discouragement dial for a moment, but this method always turns up the dial even more in the long run.

A longtime friend of mine gave me permission to share his story but not his name, so I'll call him Steve.[1] I met Steve in a men's group more than ten years ago. Steve shared regularly about some of the problems he was having in his marriage. He and his wife were continually fighting, and more often than not, the fights were about sex—or more specifically the lack of it. Steve was disappointed because what he was experiencing (really, *not* experiencing) was so much different from what he was expecting. It didn't take long for that disappointment to turn into discouragement.

---

1. I do have real friends named Steve, but this isn't about any of those actual Steves. I could have picked a name that doesn't match with anyone I know by that name—something like "Elmer." But I think using the name Elmer throughout a story is more of a distraction. Sidenote: what's ironic about the name Elmer is that it means "famous," and I can't think of any famous Elmers.

Over the next few years, Steve became more and more discouraged. He started dealing with his discouragement by doing things the anti-God way. God's way would have been to treat his wife with tenderness and put her needs ahead of his own. God's way would have called him to love her with the sacrificial love of Jesus. But he did the opposite.

First, he tried to deal with his discouragement by being demanding. He put incredible pressure on her to meet his needs, and he became angry when she refused. Then he dealt with his discouragement by becoming more and more distant. He wanted physical intimacy but was intentionally withholding emotional intimacy.

One morning, as our men's group sat around a table, Steve confessed his porn addiction. When things weren't going his way in his marriage, he started to find other ways to satisfy his desires. He knew it was wrong, but even as he confessed it, he was still blaming his wife and justifying himself.

At some point, his wife discovered his porn addiction, and they started sleeping in separate rooms. This went on for almost two years, and then one day, Steve discovered text messages between his wife and another man. She was willingly giving this other man the kind of attention Steve had demanded. He confronted her in a self-righteous rage. Eventually, she'd had enough and moved out. When Steve felt discouraged, he tried the DIY approach and allowed his discouragement to justify his disobedience—and it only made things more discouraging.

Elkanah does the same thing. When things don't go his way with Hannah, he married a second wife, Peninnah—and it only made things worse. But something else happened that always happens: his disobedience not only made things worse for him; it made things incredibly discouraging for Hannah.

Every year, Elkanah took his two wives to visit Shiloh, which was about a twenty-mile journey. First Samuel 1:6–7 (NLT) tells us that every year when they made this journey, "Peninnah would taunt Hannah and make fun of her because the LORD had kept her from having children. Year after year it was the same—Peninnah would taunt Hannah as they went to the Tabernacle. Each time, Hannah would be reduced to tears and would not even eat."

Hannah's discouragement dial gets turned up even more by a difficult person. I'm sure Hannah tried to make it work. Maybe she had even read *Have a New Sister Wife by Friday*, but nothing seemed to change.

Prolonged Disappointment

Did you catch the phrase in 1 Samuel 1:7 that serves as a pretty good definition of discouragement: *year after year it was the same*? It's not that we can't handle it for a few months or even a few years, but when it goes on "year after year" and nothing changes, we start to lose confidence. The equation looks something like this:

Disappointment + Time = Discouragement

The longer we stand in line waiting for things to go our way, the more discouraged we feel.

Hannah's situation was desperate. She was in tears and so upset that she wouldn't even eat. Some of you know that degree of discouragement. You've lost your appetite. You have trouble sleeping. Your emotional exhaustion has turned into physical exhaustion. Your troubles consume you. For a while, you could compartmentalize it, but now it's just leaking all over everything.

When enough time goes by and things aren't going our way, we often deal with that prolonged discouragement with denial.

One of the shows we watch at our house is *Shark Tank*. In the show, inventors and entrepreneurs seeking financial partners pitch their products or businesses to a group of five wealthy venture capitalists. If you've watched *Shark Tank*, you may remember an invention called the Skinny Mirror. This mirror uses curved glass to create an optical illusion, so the user will look about ten pounds thinner. It was originally designed for individuals, but the creators found that retailers were interested in using the mirror to help sell clothing. When you try on clothes at a store and use the Skinny Mirror to gauge how they fit, you're much more likely to make a purchase.

What I found especially interesting about this mirror is that the manufacturers don't try to hide what it is. In fact, they put their name right on the mirror. So the next time you're at a store trying on a pair of jeans and love what you see in the mirror, whatever you do, don't look at the bottom right-hand corner for the Skinny Mirror logo.

I was thinking someone could probably develop an entire product line around the idea that our preferred way of dealing with discouragement is denial. There could be the Skinny Scale—a complementary product to the Skinny Mirror. When you weigh yourself on this scale, it gives you a weight ten pounds lighter than reality. That way, what you see on the scale matches up with what you see in the mirror. There could also be the Skinny Glasses. You realize that your Skinny Mirror makes you look great and your Skinny Scale validates it, but what will your significant other *actually* see? Just ask them to put on a pair of the Skinny Glasses, and they'll see exactly what you want them to see.

When our way isn't working, we often try to surround ourselves with voices that tell us what we want to hear—voices that help us deal with our discouragement by reinforcing our denial.

Constant Comparisons

The closest thing I have to a superpower is the ability to always choose the longest line. Whether it's a checkout line, a drive-through, or the airport security line, I will always choose the longest line. My family knows I'm the Michael Jordan of picking the longest line, so they usually go to a different line. When it becomes clear that their line is shorter, I'm not allowed to join them because they know the force is so strong within me that the moment I get in their line, it will become longer.

Here's what I know from years and years of experience at waiting in long lines: I don't get discouraged unless I compare. If I avoid tracking the speed of my line with the line next to me, everything is fine. If I compare, I become discouraged.

The discouragement dial gets turned up when our way isn't working, but even more so when everyone else's way seems to be doing just fine.

We can call this the "Peninnah effect." It's one thing to be barren; it's quite another thing to live in the same house with your husband's other wife who is popping out kids. It was especially difficult when they would travel as one big family to Shiloh and Peninnah would rub it in Hannah's face.

In 1 Samuel 1:8 (NLT), Elkanah tries to comfort his wife: "'Why are you crying, Hannah?' Elkanah would ask." So far he's doing okay. He's asking her what's wrong and why she's feeling down. Now it's time for him to be quiet and listen. But that's not what he does. He keeps going: "Why aren't you eating? Why be downhearted just because you have no children? You have me—isn't that better than having ten sons?"

C'mon, bro, really? You have two wives, and you're still playing JV?

Elkanah could have turned down her discouragement dial if he would've only listened. Instead, he turns it up by doing two things you never want to do when someone you care about is feeling discouraged.

First, he minimizes her feelings: *Why should you be discouraged just because you have no children.* He's trying to fix this situation by pretending like it's no big deal. She already feels like something is wrong with her. Now he's trying to tell her, "There's something wrong with you for feeling like there's something wrong with you."

I hope you don't have people in your life who respond to your discouragement this way: *Oh, you feel discouraged? Let me say something that will really make you feel bad.*

Second, he makes it even worse by assuming that he's enough to make her feel better: *Aren't I worth more than ten sons? Do you know how lucky you are to be married to me? How could you ever be discouraged when you're married to such an understanding husband?*

He asks her how she feels, but then instead of listening to how she feels, he tries to fix her. This isn't an effective approach to husbanding, or so I'm told. Husbands, if you're not quite convinced, try the "Elkanah approach" and see how it works for ya. Next time your wife is upset about something, say to her, "Hey, baby, you got *me*! What more could you possibly want in life? Isn't winning the husband lottery enough for you?"

All of this ridicule and fake comfort would have made Hannah feel especially alone. And nothing turns up the discouragement dial more than loneliness. To be clear, Hannah *felt* alone but she wasn't alone. She lived in a house with a husband who minimized her, another woman who belittled her, and children who unknowingly demeaned her. You can be surrounded by people and feel alone. One time when my middle daughter was in elementary school, I asked her, "When have you felt the loneliest in your life?" And she said, "When I sat by myself at a table with all the other girls."

Hannah is discouraged, but instead of helping pull her out of it, Elkanah's insensitive comments only add to the discouragement she feels because what he says makes her discouragement feel invalid, which only makes her feel more alone.

Craving Connection

First Samuel 1:9 (NLT) reads, "Once after a sacrificial meal at Shiloh, Hannah got up and went to pray." The phrase "got up" communicates more than posture. It is not telling us she was "sitting down" and then "stood up." It's telling us she'd had enough of living that way.

You reach a point where you've tried things your way. You've attempted to fix your problem, control it, ignore it, diminish it, and dismiss it. You've even allowed yourself to wallow in it. And now it's all led to a desperate moment when you have to decide if you'll keep sitting or if you'll stand up. Hannah stood up and went to pray.

Even though Hannah stood up, she was in "deep anguish" as she "prayed to the LORD, weeping bitterly" (1 Samuel 1:10). The double use of the Hebrew *bakah* in this verse indicates more than simply the presence of tears;

it describes a loud weeping or even wailing. In addition to this image of weeping, there are six different Hebrew words used in 1 Samuel 1:1–18 to describe the discouragement that Hannah is feeling. Think of these as six different degrees on the discouragement dial:

1. Downhearted (*raa lebab*)
2. In deep anguish (*mar nephesh*)
3. In misery (*oni*)
4. Deeply troubled (*qashet ruah*)
5. In great anguish (*siyah*)
6. In grief (*kaas*)

You'll notice two different Hebrew words are translated in this passage into English as "anguish." You know why? Perhaps it's because we've run out of English words to capture the discouragement she was feeling. On the Wheel of Emotions, we find a lot of different emotions labeled as discouragement, but sometimes the level of discouragement exceeds our vocabulary. We just can't put it into words.

Hannah's discouragement leads to desperation, and in her desperation, she cries out to God. Remember, we've said that our emotions move us somewhere. In this case, Hannah allows her discouragement to drive her to connection.

We can read her prayer for connection: "O Lord of Heaven's Armies, if you will look upon my sorrow and answer my prayer and give me a son, then I will give him back to you. He will be yours for his entire lifetime, and as a sign that he has been dedicated to the LORD, his hair will never be cut" (1 Samuel 1:11 NLT). She says to God, "I will give him back to you"—which may sound like she's negotiating: "God, if you do this for me, I'll do this for you." But we can't negotiate with God. It's literally impossible. God holds all the chips. We've got nothing to offer him that he needs, and God does not negotiate with us. God isn't holding out on us until he gets what he wants. What Hannah is doing here isn't negotiating; it's *surrendering*.

This is Hannah going back out into the water and casting her nets out one more time. She's letting go of her way and surrendering to God's will.

> As she was praying to the LORD, Eli watched her. Seeing her lips moving but hearing no sound, he thought she had been drinking. "Must you come here drunk?" he demanded. "Throw away your wine!"
>
> "Oh no, sir!" she replied. "I haven't been drinking wine or anything stronger. But I am very discouraged, and I was pouring out my heart to the LORD." (1 Samuel 1:12–15 NLT)

Don't miss the description and the progression that takes place in this passage. *I was very discouraged, so I poured out my heart to God.*

And that's what you do. When your way isn't working and you feel very discouraged, the first thing you need to do is simply pour out your heart to God.

Hannah then says to Eli, "Don't think I am a wicked woman! For I have been praying out of great anguish and sorrow." To which Eli replies, "Go in peace! May the God of Israel grant the request you have asked of him." Hannah responds with gratitude and "went back and began to eat again, and she was no longer sad" (1 Samuel 1:16–18).

The order of things here is interesting. After Hannah cries out to God, she feels better. She is no longer discouraged. I have some questions for you:

> *Is she pregnant?* No.
> *Has she been promised a miracle?* No.
> *Does God speak to her in an audible voice and tell her she*
> * will conceive?* No.
> *Does God tell her she's finally going to get her way?* No.

And yet she is no longer discouraged. Don't miss this: her discouraging circumstances have not changed, but her connection with God has.

We are told that Hannah and the rest of the family returned home. After some time had passed, Hannah conceived. She was given a son, whom she named Samuel, which sounds like the Hebrew "heard by God." So now every time she said his name, she was reminded that in her discouragement God had heard her.

Discouragement is a loss of hope, but every time Hannah spoke Samuel's name, her heart was filled with hope.

Discouragement can do one of two things: it can either drive us away from God or draw us closer to him.

Maybe you find yourself on an adventure you never would have chosen, and you know you don't have the power to choose what happens next in your story. But while you can't choose your own adventures, you can choose how you will respond to them. This can be a chapter in your story where you cry out to God, put your hope in him, and then, with his strength, get up and keep moving forward.

CHAPTER 4

"I'VE HAD ENOUGH"

The Frustration Meter

Brené Brown is a sociologist and research professor at the University of Houston and an author with six number-one bestsellers. She has spent the last few decades identifying and exploring the different emotions that are part of the human experience. In her book *Atlas of the Heart*, she talks about mapping eighty-seven key emotions, but she points out that most people only identify feeling three different emotions: happy, sad, and pissed off.[1]

---

1. See Brené Brown, *Atlas of the Heart: Mapping Human Connection and the Language of Human Experience* (New York: Random House, 2022), xxi, xxiii. I want to apologize to my mom for using the phrase "pissed off." I know you would have preferred "ticked off," but I was quoting a source. Full disclosure though: Brown used the word *angry* to describe one of the three emotions.

For a long time, I would only identify myself as "happy." Growing up in the church, I picked up on this idea that the happier you are, the more spiritual you are. If you're walking through a church lobby and someone asks, "How are you?" there are three acceptable answers: "Super," "Great," and "Super Great." At the church I grew up in, one of the pastors had a collection of answers when you asked him how he was doing. Here are a few I remember:

> "If I was any more blessed, there would be two of me."
> "If I was any happier, I'd have to sit on my hands to keep from clapping."
> "If I were any better, vitamins would be taking *me*."
> "If I had a tail, I'd wag it."

So for most of my life, I really only had one emotion I would admit to—happy. My Wheel of Emotions consisted of a single spoke. In my family, when we had a bad day, instead of saying, "It's been a tough day," my dad taught us to say, "Every day is a good day, but some are better than others." And we had plenty of Scripture plaques posted around the house to remind us that God wanted us to be happy.

While I'm thankful for the joyful and positive home I grew up in, I also picked up on the fact that I was expected to be happy all the time—or at least pretend to be. In fact, my nickname as a little boy was "Kyle Smile," which as far as nicknames go could have been worse.[2]

---

2. Like when I was in high school and my nickname was "Alf," as in the comedy

In my book *Grace Is Greater*, I talked about receiving grace from my wife and Jesus when I got angry and punched a hole in the door. What I didn't include in that story was what had happened that made me angry enough to punch a hole in the door.

I had gotten into an argument with my wife, and while the details of the argument are none of your business, I'll give you the highlights: One of us wanted to make a last-minute change to our plan of driving ten hours to visit in-laws in Kansas. This very reasonable person instead wanted to drive ten hours and spend the week on white sand beaches making memories as a family. And when this very reasonable person didn't get his way, he punched the door.

"Kyle Smile" does not punch holes in doors.[3] But when his way isn't working, he acts happy as long as he can, but eventually he loses it. He has now discovered that his level of frustration with people or circumstances is one of the reliable ways he can gauge how connected he is to Jesus.

The less I'm abiding in Jesus, the more easily annoyed I am by others.

The less time I spend remaining in him, the less patience I have in me.

The First Frustration

The first time we see anger in the Bible is in Genesis 4. Adam and Eve have two sons: Cain and Abel. The story goes like this:

---

sitcom about Alf the Alien Life Form. It was because I was so hairy.

3. Kyle Volatile or Kyle Imbecile—yes, but not quite as catchy.

Now Abel kept flocks, and Cain worked the soil. In the course of time Cain brought some of the fruits of the soil as an offering to the Lord. And Abel also brought an offering—fat portions from some of the firstborn of his flock. The Lord looked with favor on Abel and his offering, but on Cain and his offering he did not look with favor. (Genesis 4:2–5)

Notice that God looks first at the person and then at the offering. He knows the motives of a person's heart. The indication here is that Abel has a connection with God and that his offering reflects it. Abel gives the fat portions from the firstborn of his flock. In other words, he gives God the best of what he has.

Cain also gives to God, but it is more from the leftovers. In essence, Abel says, "Before I do anything else, I'm going to give to God." Cain does things his way, saying essentially, "I'll see what's left over and give that to God." God accepts Abel's offering and blesses him, but he rejects Cain's offering. And so "Cain was very angry, and his face was downcast" (Genesis 4:5). Two of our identified emotions are referenced here. He's discouraged and angry. It's unclear if Cain knows that's what he's feeling. So God points it out and asks him why he's feeling that way:

Then the Lord said to Cain, "Why are you angry? Why is your face downcast? If you do what is right, will you not be accepted? But if you do not do what is right, sin is crouching at your door; it desires to have you, but you must rule over it."

Now Cain said to his brother Abel, "Let's go out to the field." While they were in the field, Cain attacked his brother Abel and killed him. (Genesis 4:6–8)

When God asks Cain the question, "Why are you angry?" he's asking Cain to stop, look, and examine his feelings. "Don't just feel your feelings, Cain. Ask yourself *why* you feel the way you feel. Where is the anger coming from?"

One of the reasons that's a good question is that not all anger is bad. Paul wrote in Ephesians 4:26, "In your anger do not sin." The King James Version put it this way: "Be ye angry, and sin not." "Be ye angry" is an imperative, but this verse makes it clear that it's possible to be angry without sinning. Anger generally comes because we want things to go our way and they're not, but feeling anger can be righteous if it comes from our desire to have things God's way. We read about the way Jesus got angry and overturned the tables in the temple. We read several times about his anger with religious leaders. But don't miss this: his anger wasn't a selfish "I want things my way" kind of anger; it was a protective anger. He didn't get angry when people hurt him or treated him unfairly; no, he got angry when others—especially the vulnerable—were taken advantage of.

Why was Cain angry? We're not given the specific reason. However, at least one thing seems clear: he is jealous of his brother and doesn't seem to think he is being treated fairly.

My guess is that what we read in Genesis 4 is a tipping point for Cain. There has likely been a long history between these brothers. Maybe Cain, the older brother, felt like Abel was always getting the favored treatment he felt he deserved as the older brother.

It's Not You, It's Me

Cain is angry with Abel, or at least he thinks he is, but here's a question: *What did Abel to do him?*

Ummm . . . *nothing.*

Abel didn't do anything to him. I think Cain was actually angry with himself. His way wasn't working and he knew it, but instead of looking in the mirror and asking himself some hard questions, he directed his anger toward Abel.

As a young couple, when my wife and I moved into our first real neighborhood, I discovered that the guy next door took immaculate care of his lawn. No dandelions or weeds or dry patches. His grass had that checkered pattern that to me is a clear indication that someone is involved in the dark arts. When we would pass our neighbor's yard, my wife would admire his lawn and point out how good it looked. I had only met my neighbor a time or two, but I thought to myself, *I can't stand that guy.*

What did my neighbor do to me? Nothing. Yet his grass was an indictment of me. I couldn't drive by his yard without being reminded that my way wasn't working. And by my way, I mean pretending like dandelions are beautiful flowers.

I was annoyed with him, but really, I was annoyed with me. I think that's part of the dynamic we witness between Cain and Abel. Cain takes his anger out on Abel, but I wonder if he's really angry with himself. Anger with ourselves over our failures and shortcomings often comes out sideways and gets redirected to the people around us.

Anger is often described as a secondary emotion. You show anger, but maybe what you really feel is fear. You're afraid your way isn't going to work and you're going to fail—in your marriage, as a parent, at work. It's much easier to be angry than to admit we're scared of failing. The more disconnected we are from Jesus, the more dependent we become on ourselves, and the more we depend on ourselves, the more we fear failure—and this is a fear that surfaces as anger.

Or maybe you show anger, but what you're really feeling is shame. It's natural to feel shame when our way isn't working. I think Cain felt some shame around his offering, but it was easier to become angry and blame his brother. Instead of taking responsibility and humbling himself, Cain deals with his shame by becoming angry. God tells Cain, "If you do what is right, will you not be accepted?" (Genesis 4:7). Cain can humble himself and do what is right, or he can be defensive and angry.

Or perhaps you display anger, but what you really are is just plain tired. You're overwhelmed, and the more tired and frustrated you become, the shorter your fuse gets. These are the days when you wake up angry and anything or anyone becomes a source of irritation. You lash out, and you're not even sure where *that* came from.

Reading the Meter

Genesis 4:8 reveals the horrible result: "Now Cain said to his brother Abel, 'Let's go out to the field.' While they were in the field, Cain attacked his brother Abel and killed him."

When some people get angry, you know it. They express their anger in a dramatic and sometimes even violent way. I once read about a guy named Justin John Boudin, a twenty-seven-year-old man from Minnesota, who lost his temper one day, which led to fifth-degree assault charges. Sadly, assaults happen every day, but what made Justin's story a news story is that when he committed this crime, he was on his way to an anger management class. Apparently, he was at a bus stop waiting to catch a ride to his anger management class when he got into an argument with a fifty-nine-year-old woman.

Justin felt disrespected. She pulled out her cell phone to call the police. He punched her in the face. As a sixty-three-year-old man tried to intervene, Justin hit the man with the blue folder he was holding. He then dropped the folder and ran away. When police examined the contents of the blue folder, they discovered it contained Justin's homework from his anger management class—the one he was on his way to attend.[4]

---

4. See Associated Press, "Man Hits Woman on Way to Anger Control Class," *Today*, March 1, 2008, www.today.com/id/wbna23421960.

Even though he was on his way to an anger management class, Justin wasn't able to control his temper, and that impulsiveness got him into even more trouble. I'm sure he wasn't planning on losing control in that moment, but anger has a way of sneaking up on us. It shows up when our way isn't working and makes things even worse.

Some of you read the story of Cain and hear about Justin and you think, *Well, that's not me. I don't lose my temper.* You think of anger as what's displayed by someone who yells and screams and calls names and throws things across the room—and punches holes in doors. *You* would never do those things, so it may be harder to spot your anger.

Perhaps when you get angry, you don't flip out and get violent; rather, you become manipulative. You express your anger by making yourself the victim. You try to get everyone to feel sorry for you. Some of you express your anger through sarcasm, so you can say hurtful things. You cowardly hide behind saying things like, "I'm just joking. Don't be so sensitive."

Maybe you're passive-aggressive. You withhold attention, affection, and encouragement until you get what you want. When someone asks if something's wrong, you continue to play games and say, "Everything's fine."

Or you might be one who stonewalls. You withdraw from a person. Ignoring someone or giving them the silent treatment is actually one of cruelest expressions of anger in close relationships. You don't have a violent explosion; instead you're like a silent assassin. You don't make much noise, but the body count of people who have crossed you is significant. You might not do what Cain did, but your anger is slowly killing the people around you.

There are many different stages of anger. Depending on where you look, you can find up to ten of them. But I'm going to boil them down into four stages.

First is *mild irritation*. It stems from things like loud kids in the house. A charging cord that mysteriously stops working during the night. Rude treatment from a coworker you don't know very well. Being compelled to watch a decorating show while a football game is on a different channel. All mild situations that can quickly add up.

Mild irritation often leads to the next stage of anger—*provoked frustration*. This is a deeper level of intensity that feels like something more intentional and spiteful. When someone cuts you off, it's a mild irritation, but when someone in a Hummer with a Duke Blue Devils bumper sticker cuts you off, it feels much more provoking.

The third stage is *personal indignation*. This is that feeling of being personally disrespected—personally attacked or intentionally mistreated. The problem is that many of us live in this stage. We have a short fuse because we skip over irritation and frustration and go straight to indignation.

We'll call the fourth stage *uncontrolled rage*. This is the action stage. The floodgates have opened and you can't tell the water where to go. You're beginning to lose the ability to think rationally about what you should say or how you should respond. Physically, when you get angry, your rational prefrontal lobe begins to shut down and the reflexive back areas of your brain start to take over. The left hemisphere of your brain becomes more stimulated as the brain's hormonal and cardiovascular responses kick in. The flow of blood is diverted to your muscles, preparing your body for action. At this stage, you are capable of saying things and doing things you never thought you would say or do.

Our challenge is to pay close attention to our anger. While things are still in the irritation or frustration stage, we must take a breath and connect with the Vine.

Crouching at the Door

Here's what's interesting: before Cain loses control, God warns him about what's going to happen if he keeps doing things his way. God says, "If you refuse to do what is right, then watch out! Sin is crouching at the door, eager to control you" (Genesis 4:7 NLT).

God tells Cain to watch out. So it may be for you as well. You may not see it coming, but sin's control is coming quickly. Your anger is a warning, like a flashing light on the dashboard of your car, letting you know your way isn't working. If you keep going, you're going to walk through a door you won't be able to walk back through.

Bob Merritt is a friend of mine who served as the pastor of Eagle Brook Church in Minnesota for years. He wrote about what he called his "leadership meltdown." Bob felt overworked and overwhelmed. Cracks started showing up in harsh comments and bursts of anger toward his family and coworkers. Emotionally, he felt depleted. But he told himself he didn't have the time or energy to address the issues bubbling under the surface. Finally, his church board forced him to look under the surface by entering into a yearlong intervention with a leadership coach named Fred. Bob writes about his experience:

> Fred and his assistant interviewed all my family members, most of my staff, and all of my closest friends with a series of 60 questions that essentially asked, "What's good about Bob, and what's bad about Bob?" The candid responses were recorded in a 200-page document that Fred and his assistant read back to me, word for word, during a two-day intervention.
>
> For two solid days I sat and listened while Fred read statements like: "Bob overlooks relationships and lacks interpersonal skills in working with people." "Bob doesn't listen well." "Bob doesn't manage his staff. There's no love. He's unapproachable." "Bob speaks before he thinks." "Bob has a love problem." "I know that Bob cares, but he's not gifted in showing it." . . .
>
> What really nailed me was when I heard these words from my son, David: "My dad is angry a lot." When Fred read those words to me, he looked up from the page and just let them sink into my soul. I had to look away. . . .
>
> When you hear the same themes repeated over and over again from a variety of people who've experienced

what it's like to be on the other side of you, it gets your attention. . . .

It broke me.

And it was the beginning of my new life.[5]

"When I first started seeing Fred," Bob writes, "I told him I was afraid I might not be able to change. Fred has seen hundreds of leaders, and he says the success rate is only around 40 percent. The other 60 percent continue to stumble and often end up losing their jobs and families. He said the difference is humility. Those who turn the corner and take their leadership and lives to a new level are those who are humble enough to receive feedback and take it seriously."[6]

So if you're worn-out, confused, afraid, or a bit paranoid about what others are saying about you; if you're angry, bitter, lonely, or misunderstood; when your anger makes it clear that your way isn't working, I urge you to ask yourself a vital question: *Am I humble enough to address the cracks?*

In Genesis 4, God puts a heavy hand on the door that Cain is about to walk through. God warns Cain to pay attention to the anger he feels and not to keep going down that path. Look at your dashboard. Check your frustration meter. It's one of the most accurate indicators of a disconnected life. The question is this: *Are you going to keep doing things your way?*

---

5. Bob Merritt, "Ministry Meltdown," SmallGroups.com, Christianity Today, 3–6, https://cornerstonechurch.ca/wp-content/uploads/2020/09/Avoiding-Burnout .pdf.
6. Merritt, "Ministry Meltdown," 6.

Bob Merritt's story was published in *Leadership Journal* in 2012, but I came across it in 2020.[7] As I read the story, I kept thinking, *This must be a different Bob Merritt from the one I know.* I became friends with Bob four or five years ago. He had retired from his role as senior pastor at Eagle Brook, but he has been a pastor to me. He has gone out of his way to encourage me and challenge me. When I visit with him, he's always willing to share, humbly and vulnerably, the variety of struggles he had in ministry.

Recently, I had dinner with him and told him about reading the article. I said, "When I read it, I kept thinking, *This must be a different Bob Merritt because I don't know this guy.*" Bob spent the rest of our meal encouraging me and empathizing with the challenges I was going through. He prayed for me and made sure I knew he was available if I needed anything.

Bob's way simply wasn't working. The busyness and demands of his role made it difficult to find the time and emotional energy to connect deeply with Jesus and others. Over time, his frustration meter started to tell a story. His anger started spilling out onto the people around him. But as he focused on his connection with Jesus, he was humble enough to address the cracks. Through his connection with Jesus, he found the grace to be honest with himself and the strength to start doing things differently.

A few months after my dinner with Bob, I sat down for

---

7. See Merritt, "Ministry Meltdown."

a meeting with a couple of the leaders I serve with at church who had some concerns they wanted to share. That's not surprising; the majority of my meetings are with people who want to "share some concerns." What made this meeting different is that the concerns they had were about *me*. It had been an exhausting season of ministry navigating significant transitions in our church and the challenges of the COVID-19 pandemic. These leaders sensed that the exhaustion of the season was causing me to become more easily annoyed with people. One of them said, "You seem angry." I was immediately defensive. "I'm not angry; I'm just frustrated." I went on to list all the things I was entitled to be frustrated about.

Instead of humbly receiving their concerns and setting aside time to check for cracks, I demanded examples of what they were talking about. "Have I ever raised my voice? Have I ever lost my temper? Give me some examples of how I've been sarcastic or harsh?" I was starting to get . . . well . . . frustrated. When I finished, they both sat in silence for a few moments. I took a breath and realized that this was what they were talking about.

One of them said, "It's not so much what you've said or done that we can point to; it's more the look you have on your face right now." There was no mirror around, but I didn't need one. Apparently my RPF[8] wasn't communicating the gentle kindness that tends to flow when the branch is connected with the Vine.

---

8. Resting Pastor Face.

As I sat in that meeting, I remembered the words of my friend Bob. I asked myself the question, *Am I humble enough to address the cracks?* My way wasn't working, and now God was using these two leaders to put a hand on the door and warn me before I went any farther.

My prayer is that this chapter will do the same for you. Maybe you don't have someone in your life who has the courage or the permission to speak freely to you, but you know you've been on edge. The people around you may not be saying anything, but it's because they know you'll be defensive and overreact. But maybe the truth is that the people closest to you feel like they're living next to a volcano. They never know what's going to upset you or set you off. Instead of minimizing your frustration or justifying it, what if you humbly acknowledged it?

What if you found time to take a breath and listen to God?

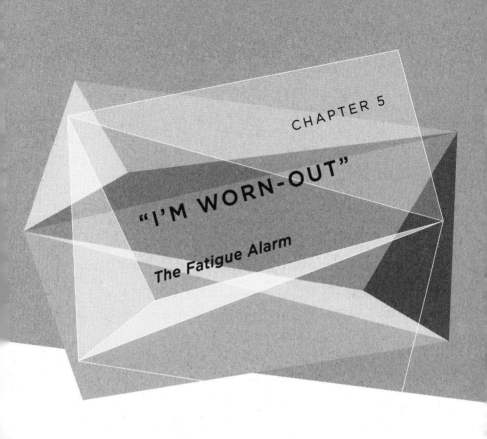

CHAPTER 5

"I'M WORN-OUT"

The Fatigue Alarm

t takes a lot to get me to go see a doctor. It's not that I don't like my doctor; he's actually a friend of mine. I enjoy having lunch with him and trading funny memes. I just don't especially enjoy going to see him when something is wrong with me. Before an appointment, I'll usually shoot him a text that begins with, "I'm sure it's no big deal . . ." Then he will encourage me to come in so he can take a look. I typically let him know I'm a little busy for the next few weeks, but when things slow down, I'll make an appointment.

Last year, we had a text conversation that went something like this:

ME: Hey, Doc, I'm not sure what's wrong, but I haven't been myself lately and I can't stop yawning.

DOCTOR: I think I know what it might be. Tell me more.

ME: Well, I wake up feeling groggy and unmotivated. And lately I've been more easily irritated with people.

DOCTOR: Are you getting enough sleep and taking some time off?

ME: 😬

DOCTOR: How's your diet and exercise routine?

ME: How's your fasting and tithing routine?

DOCTOR: I think I'm ready to make a diagnosis.

ME: *bracing myself*

DOCTOR: You're tired.

ME: 🙄

When he told me I was tired, it sent me down a Google rabbit trail of what makes someone feel tired. There were a lot of possibilities—nutrient deficiencies, thyroid problems, hormone imbalance, adrenal gland issues, perimenopause. There had to be some explanation.

After some research, I texted my doctor to let him know what I discovered. Doctors love it when a patient spends an hour on Google and questions their expert diagnosis. I went through the list of the potential medical conditions that I thought might be causing me to feel so tired. I was hoping for a prescription to fix the problem. He told me to come in and he'd run some tests. He hooked me up to some different machines and ordered a bunch of blood work.

When the results came in, he called to let me know I was completely healthy. All my numbers and levels were right where they should be. It didn't make sense to me because I knew something was wrong. He told me he was ready to give me his official diagnosis and course of treatment: *You're tired and need to rest.*

My body had reached a point where it couldn't keep doing things my way. My way was to never slow down. When my wife, kids, or friends would tell me I needed to take a break, I had a go-to answer: *It's a busy season.*

The problem was that it had been a busy season *for the past four years.* It got to the point where my friends and family began joking about my "it's a busy season" answer.

Around that same time, a friend of mine texted and said he had listened to a helpful sermon on rest that he wanted to send to me. His next text read, "Even though it's a busy season, will you commit to listening to the message I'm going to send you?" I told him I would, and he texted me a link to the sermon. It was a sermon I had preached a few years earlier on the importance of rest.

I was starting to get the message. I was too busy and too distracted, and my schedule wasn't only making me tired; it was keeping me from being deeply connected with Jesus and the people around me. "It's a busy season" had gone on for too long. I was about to be given an off-season, whether I wanted one or not.

Just One More Thing

My way that wasn't working was defined by having good intentions but not being very intentional. I had good intentions of living life with enough margin to stay deeply connected with Jesus and others, but when a new opportunity or worthwhile request came along, I'd usually say yes—and think to myself, *It's just one more thing.* And it's not like that one more thing was going to kill me, so it would get added onto the schedule.

My "just one more thing" way of life wasn't working. There is a compounding effect to our schedules. You may be adding one more thing to your calendar, which doesn't seem significant on its own, but it makes everything else feel heavier.

I was recently spotting a buddy at the gym who was going for a personal best for his bench press. He lay down on the bench, ready to remove the bar from the supports and lower it to his chest. He had successfully completed 225 and was now attempting 230. He had me add two-and-a-half-pound plates to each side. That's didn't seem significant. Not to brag, but I could hold it up using a pinky. He lifted the bar off the support and slowly lowered it to his chest, but when he tried to press it back up, he couldn't do it. It was too much. He grunted out the word *spot* to let me know he needed some help. The two-and-a-half-pound plates weren't significant on their own, but when they got added to the rest of the plates on the bar, it was too much.

Think of your schedule as a bar with weights that you need to bench-press. Bench-pressing one plate at a time wouldn't be difficult, but that's not how it works. The plates are separate, but once a plate is added to the bar, the whole thing gets heavier. So imagine a bar with a series of weights representing your schedule. The forty-five-pound plate represents a full-time job. The thirty-five-pound plate represents your responsibilities at home. The twenty-pound plate represents the time you've set aside to exercise and stay in shape. The ten-pound plate represents your commitment to volunteer at church, and the five-pound weight is the one you added to the bar when you started to run the car pool three days a week. Any one of those plates is manageable on its own, but as they're added to the bar, the whole thing becomes heavier.

The tendency is to underestimate the compounding effect that adding one more thing has on the whole, with the result that at some point the bar becomes too heavy.

Speed of Life

It's not just "the more" that wears us out; it's the speed by which we live. The problem is we keep adding more and doing it faster. *More* and *faster* may be the words that mark our lives, but connections require *margin* and *time*.

A buddy of mine was telling me his second-grade daughter asked if she could join the swim team. When he asked her why, she said she wanted to have fun with her friends. That

75

made sense to my friend because his daughter had never been very competitive. He thought an experience like this might help light a competitive fire, so he and his wife agreed she could be on the team.

He watched the first few swim meets, and it was pretty painful. His daughter came in close to last place in every race. But it didn't seem to bother her, and that bothered him. He was glad she was having a great time, but she didn't look like she even cared about winning. One day after a meet, he asked her, "Are you giving it your very best and going as fast as you can when you're out there?"

He was not prepared for her honest answer. "Not really. I'm just having fun swimming with my friends." At some point in the conversation, my friend realized something: his daughter didn't understand it was a race. Somehow no one had made it clear that the objective was to try to swim faster than everyone else. She thought being on the swim team meant you jumped in the water with your friends and swam to the other end of the pool. She had no idea she was supposed to be racing them.

My buddy suddenly had a decision to make: Should he tell her? Should he tell her it's a race to see who's the fastest? Should he tell her that whether or not she is good is determined by how many seconds it takes her to get to the finish line? Should he tell her she needs to go as fast as she can—and that going faster than everyone else means she's the best? Or should he just let her jump in the pool and have fun swimming back and forth with her friends? Well, of course he told her. He said something like this: "It's a race, and if you want to be on the swim team, you'd better start treating it like one."

My buddy's daughter wasn't interested in going fast. She just wanted to have fun with her friends. Yet the purpose for being on the team wasn't supposed to be connecting with others; it was to go as fast as she could so she could be better and more successful than everyone else.

As we get older, we keep choosing more and faster over relationships, and it's clear that this approach to life isn't working. As a pastor, I've often officiated funerals for people who made their lives about winning the race. They pushed themselves to be stronger and faster and measured themselves by medals and ribbons—but at what cost? Too often, they had little time left over for connecting with friends and family who were in the water with them.

Dr. Suzanne Koven is an internist at Massachusetts General Hospital. In 2013, she wrote a piece in the *Boston Globe* about an "epidemic" she was seeing with her patients:

> In the past few years, I've observed an epidemic of sorts: patient after patient suffering from the same condition. The symptoms of this condition include fatigue, irritability, insomnia, anxiety, headaches, heartburn, bowel disturbances, back pain, and weight gain. There are no blood tests or X-rays diagnostic of this condition, and yet it's easy to recognize. The condition is excessive busyness.[1]

---

1. Suzanne Koven, "Busy Is the New Sick," *Boston Globe*, July 23, 2013, http://archive.boston.com/lifestyle/health/blog/inpractice/2013/07/busy_is_the_new_sick.html.

Excessive busyness is truly an epidemic—a widespread epidemic that has been around for quite a while.

In the Old Testament, we discover that Elijah is realizing that his way isn't working. In 1 Kings 19:4, we read, "He came to a broom bush, sat down under it and prayed that he might die. 'I have had enough, LORD,' he said. 'Take my life.'"

Elijah is worn-out to the point of feeling despair. He's so overwhelmed that he tells God he can't take any more suffering and that his life isn't worth living. To understand how Elijah got there, we have to hit rewind and go back about three and a half years.

Elijah warned King Ahab that because of the nation's sin and rebellion against God, God was going to cause a drought in the land. Ahab didn't take it seriously. But one day of no rain turned into another and another. Everything happened exactly as Elijah said it would, and he had to run for his life and hide.

During that time, a lot of people didn't like Elijah. They blamed him for the drought. So Elijah was always on the run, paranoid that someone was going to find him and kill him.

The prolonged drought ended quite dramatically. You may be familiar with the story. Elijah came out of hiding and challenged 450 false prophets to a contest to determine the one true God. He met them on Mount Carmel and invited them to make an altar to their god—to Baal—and Elijah would make an altar to his God. Then they'd each call on their deities to see which one would bring fire to the altar (see 1 Kings 18:22–24).

The prophets of Baal begged and pleaded with their false god. They even cut themselves trying to get their gods' attention. Eventually, Elijah started to trash-talk. The prophets finally gave up, and it was Elijah's turn. He decided to make the contest even more challenging, and so he had them drench the altar in water. He prayed a simple prayer, and suddenly God sent a fire down from heaven that consumed the altar. The huge crowd that had gathered gell to their knees and began to worship God.

Elijah told King Ahab that because the people repented and turned to God, the drought would end and God would send a refreshing rain. Everything happened just as Elijah had predicted. Elijah was so filled with the power of God that he ran all the way to Jezreel in a rainstorm—a distance of eighteen miles.

All of that serves as a setup for this moment in 1 Kings 19 when Elijah sat under a broom bush and told God he'd had enough. For more than three years, Elijah persevered. For more than three years, he had been used in *powerful ways*. For more than three years, he stood strong. For more than three years, he had faced overwhelming odds. He was finally vindicated through a huge victory. This should have been a time of energy and refreshment. Instead, Elijah was completely burned-out. His exhaustion had left him depressed and desperate.

We discover a number of factors that contributed to Elijah's fatigue:

Extended isolation. Elijah had spent a lot of time by

himself running and hiding from others. Spending time alone may sound replenishing, and it can be for a time, but anyone who has spent much time by themselves knows how tiring that becomes. We weren't made for isolation. Social distancing may seem relaxing initially, but eventually it leaves most people feeling tired and depressed.

Difficult conversations. It's emotionally draining to have hard conversations, which is why most of us avoid them. Elijah stood in front of King Ahab and told him that God was going to send a drought. Such a conversation meant Elijah would be living under constant threat for the foreseeable future.

Strained relationships. It wasn't just the king who didn't like Elijah. Many people, even his own people, blamed him for their situation. Elijah was simply being obedient to God, but doing what God wants us to do, even when it upsets people around us, is tiring.

Prolonged uncertainty. What also depleted Elijah was that he didn't know how long the drought would last. It's one thing to go through something difficult if we know when it's going to end, but not knowing how long we have to hang on makes it much harder.

Spiritual warfare. Elijah stood alone against the false prophets. He prayed and asked God for help. This circumstance required tremendous faith. It was an incredibly intense situation that would have left him feeling emotionally and spiritually drained.

Physical exertion. On top of everything else, Elijah had run eighteen miles.[2] His body was completely exhausted. Even now, you may be thinking, *If I can just get through this, my life is going to get easier.* You keep running. You don't stop. You push through the challenge, hoping beyond hope that relief will be on the other side, but your energy is shot and you feel empty.

Mountain Moment

You may not think a great victory would be exhausting, but it's not uncommon to find yourself in a valley of fatigue after you've experienced success on the mountaintop. We see this with Olympic athletes. They train for years with a hyper-focus on one moment of competition. But after the event, even if they did incredibly well, they often hit a wall and feel completely spent, which leaves them vulnerable to depression.

Michael Phelps is the most decorated Olympian of all time, but what's left to accomplish after you've proved you're the best in the world? In the 2020 documentary *The Weight of Gold*, Phelps takes a long look at life after the Olympics and how he wasn't alone in experiencing depression after winning it all. Phelps says, "We're just so lost. A good 80 percent, maybe more, develop a post-Olympic depression."[3]

---

2. Realize this: Elijah ran for about two and a half hours and burned close to two thousand calories, and he's not running on a track, wearing Hokas, eating Cliff Bars, and stopping for Gatorade.
3. Quoted in *The Weight of Gold* (2020), dir. Brett Rapkin.

A Sense of Futility

There is nothing more tiring than giving it all we've got, only to discover it didn't make much difference. Elijah tries to be positive, but he is constantly getting discouraging news. First Kings 19:1–2 reads, "Now Ahab told Jezebel everything Elijah had done and how he had killed all the prophets with the sword. So Jezebel sent a messenger to Elijah to say, 'May the gods deal with me, be it ever so severely, if by this time tomorrow I do not make your life like that of one of them.'" Jezebel took a contract out on Elijah's life. Elijah must have thought, *Nothing has changed. Jezebel is still running the country. I just had this big victory, and now we're right back where we started.*

When your way isn't working, you feel that nothing you do matters. You're not making a difference, so it doesn't take long for the fatigue alarm to start going off.

You try to make your marriage better, you put in all the work, but a week later, nothing seems to have changed. You've tried and tried and tried. But things always seem to end up in the same place. The same arguments. The same accusations. The same stonewalling. No matter what you try, nothing seems to work.

You try to get ahead financially, and just about the time you start to make progress in eliminating debt, the car breaks down and you're facing a huge repair bill.

You try to make some changes as a parent. You read a parenting book or listen to a podcast. You try to do things differently. But the kids keep arguing and complaining, and after three or four days, you feel like you've got nothing to show for it. Things are the way they've always been, and now you're exhausted.

The Enemy of Connection

Just like someone else I know, Elijah underestimated what he had been dealing with for the past three and half years—he was tired. What he did next didn't help. He did what most of us feel like doing when we're tired: instead of connecting with others, he disconnected. First Kings 19:3–4 reads, "Elijah was afraid and ran for his life. When he came to Beersheba in Judah, he left his servant there, while he himself went a day's journey into the wilderness."

Elijah was tired and didn't feel like being around anyone else, so he disconnected and went off by himself. When your way isn't working and you feel exhausted and depressed, sometimes what you most need is what you least want. He has no energy for others, but what he doesn't need is too much time alone.

Maybe your family just moved and you don't know anyone yet. Or maybe you are reading this in the quiet of your own apartment where you live by yourself and you'll turn on the TV not because you want to watch anything but because it helps you feel less alone. Or maybe you live in a house and share a bed with a spouse, but you feel like you are married to someone who doesn't know you or understand you or accept you. Or maybe you don't have many friends right now, and as lonely as you are, the last thing you feel like doing is making new friends. You just don't have the energy for it.

When we're worn-out, it's difficult to maintain connections. We're too tired to make that kind of time or give that kind of energy. The *Seattle Times* reported on a study conducted by the UCLA Center on Everyday Lives of Families.[4] It was a four-year observation of thirty-two families. The families were observed and recorded on video for more than sixteen hundred hours at different times and in different environments. The researchers were struck at the hectic pace at which people lived their lives. Even though these families often had highly structured schedules, they had very little time or emotional energy for each other.

The video was rolling as a man walked into the bedroom after work. The kids were already in bed and his wife was folding laundry. No kiss, not even a hello. Instead, they resumed their breakfast argument virtually in midsentence over who had left the food on the counter.[5]

A mother was recorded getting ready in the morning, clearly in a hurry to head to the office. Her young daughter refused to look up and say goodbye. Finally, the embarrassed nanny prodded the girl to speak. The daughter said goodbye but never looked up.

The cameras recorded a large man entering a cramped

---

4. See Joseph B. Verrengia, "American Families' Plight: Lives Structured to a Fault," *Seattle Times*, March 20, 2005, www.seattletimes.com/nation-world/american -families-plight-lives-structured-to-a-fault.

5. By the way, he's the one who left the food on the counter.

home office where his son was playing a computer game with two buddies. He rubbed his son's head, but the boy didn't even blink. The father turned to leave, and the son pointed to the computer and muttered, "I thought you were going to fix this thing."

The UCLA study found that very few people had any unstructured time. In only one of the thirty-two families did a father regularly take an evening walk with his family. Five of the families were never in the same room at one time. The conclusion: these busy families are living at such a hectic pace with such demanding schedules that they have very little time or energy for connection.

Busyness is the enemy of connection.

Elijah's fatigue alarm is blaring but even though he doesn't seem to hear it, God hears it and takes care of Elijah by helping him rest and reconnect.

First Kings 19:5–6 tells us that Elijah "lay down under the bush and fell asleep. All at once an angel touched him and said, 'Get up and eat.' He looked around, and there by his head was some bread baked over hot coals, and a jar of water. He ate and drank and then lay down again."

God is so tender and patient with Elijah. He lets him rest. Sometimes when your way isn't working, the most spiritual thing you can do is take a nap. Elijah sleeps, and then he eats and drinks and goes back to sleep. Notice that God doesn't say, "You're burning daylight" or "You can sleep when you die." From the beginning of creation, rest has always been God's way.

It wasn't long after my doctor diagnosed me with fatigue that I sat down with my fellow leaders and told them, "I need a break." Truthfully, they already knew it. In fact, in hindsight, it's clear they knew it before I did. They could see my way wasn't working. The pace I was running was not sustainable. It's probably fair to say I was one of the last people to realize that my fatigue was affecting my connection with God and others. I was too busy to notice it.

I thought a month of rest and recovery from what had been an incredibly draining three and a half years would be plenty. After praying about it, the leaders came back and said that three months would be better. I wanted one month, and now it was three months?&!*%

At first, I resisted that length of time for all kinds of reasons. I'll give you my top three:

1. What was I going to do for three months? I was sure I would quickly get bored and restless.
2. I was embarrassed. I'm supposed to be the pastor who helps *other* people learn how to honor a commitment to prioritizing connection with Jesus and others.
3. What would happen while I was taking a break? I was sure all kinds of problems would ensue.

When I told my wife about the three-months recommendation, she said, "Thank God." And it wasn't the "thank God" you say when you've been driving around a crowded parking lot and suddenly see an empty space. It was the "thank God" someone says when she has been praying for a long time about the unsustainable pace of a loved one's life. God was answering her prayers.[6] And when I talked to one of my accountability partners, he said, "You are resisting a gift when you should be receiving it with gratitude." So that's what I did.

At first, I struggled with the lack of productivity. My therapist said, "You'll know you're doing this right when you feel unproductive." When I prayed and asked Jesus about it, here's what he said: "Are you tired? Worn out? Burned out on religion? Come to me. Get away with me and you'll recover your life. I'll show you how to take a real rest. Walk with me and work with me—watch how I do it. Learn the unforced rhythms of grace" (Matthew 11:28–29 MSG). So that's what I did. During those three months, I walked more than two hundred miles around our farm.[7]

As I connected more deeply with Jesus, I slowly began to recover my life and learn the unforced rhythms of grace.

---

6. Note: She did follow up "thank God" with "Wait, does this mean you're going to be at home all the time?" If you read that question with excitement, go back and try again.

7. I stopped keeping track because it was starting to become more about production: *How many miles can I walk in three months?* More than you, I bet.

CHAPTER 6

"I DON'T KNOW WHAT TO DO"

The Anxiety Alert

How's your way working?

I know a lot of different readers have a lot of different things going on in their lives. I'm just wondering how your way is working for you? I know some of you are married, but a lot of you aren't married. What if you never get married? Have you ever thought of that? What if your way leaves you single for the rest of your life on earth?

Or what if you get married and wish you were still single?

Or what if the person you were supposed to marry already married someone else?

Or what if you believe you've married the wrong

person? Doesn't that necessarily mean you'll end up having the wrong kids?

Or what if you marry the right person and have the right kids, but you live in the wrong city?

Or what if you marry the right person, have the right kids, and live in the right city, but you send the kids to the wrong school?

Or what if you have the right spouse and the right kids and the right city and the right school—but the wrong career? What are you supposed to do now? You can't quit. You have a spouse and kids. You've got a house payment, car insurance, student loans, and a coffee habit you have to feed. How are you gonna pay for your kids' braces? If you can't pay for your kids' braces, then they'll end up marrying the wrong person, and they'll have the wrong kids, which means eventually you'll have the wrong grandkids. And that's an awkward conversation to have with grandkids.

But you can't think about any of that right now. You probably shouldn't even be reading this book because you have all kinds of emails to respond to and text messages you're behind on. And what about your retirement plan? How's that going? You'd be a millionaire by now if you just saved the money from your coffee habit. It's too late now, so you may as well get a grande with a double shot of caffeine. You're gonna need it since you'll be working for the rest of your life.

So how's your way working for you?

One of the most predictable emotions that surfaces when

we're not living a connected life is anxiety. Typical symptoms of anxiety are fear, nervousness, irritability, sleeplessness, and the feeling of being overwhelmed. But the list of symptoms caused by anxiety can go on and on—breathing difficulties, chest pain, concentration problem, digestive issues, headaches, insomnia, muscle tension, and low energy. Anxiety can also cause memory loss and forgetfulness and insomnia, muscle tension and memory loss and forgetfulness.

Anxiety can have a strong effect on other emotions. It often surfaces in agitation, anger, and annoyance. It can make us feel moody, lonely, sad, and depressed.

For some people, anxiety is more likely to present with physical symptoms. I have a friend who says he never *feels* anxious. He would say he doesn't feel stressed, but he has migraines and hypertension and blood pressure issues. Anxiety can contribute to weight gain or loss and can even cause body odor, hair loss, and excessive armpit sweat.

The long list of anxiety symptoms includes ringing in the ears, increased sensitivity to sound and smell, and "bad taste in mouth." The list goes on, but the point is that when the anxiety alert is going off, it's best not to plug your ears and ignore it.

I know most of us aren't waking up in the morning and purposefully ignoring God's way while consciously deciding, *I'm going to do things my way.* We don't always realize that's the path we're on, so when we start to consistently feel anxious, we're being alerted to stop and consider whose way we are following.

It's not surprising that anxiety is one of the warning signs that our way isn't working. The reason some of those questions about what might or might not happen in the future create anxiety isn't just that we are uncertain about the future; it's also the weight of knowing how little control we have over what happens.

Dr. Edward Hallowell is a psychiatrist who gives this equation for anxiety (or toxic worry, as Hallowell calls it)[1]:

$$\text{Heightened Vulnerability} + \text{Lack of Control} = \text{Toxic Worry}$$

Anytime we find ourselves in a situation or facing a future in which we feel especially vulnerable and we can't do much about it, we can expect to feel some level of anxiety. We start to feel anxious *when our way isn't working*, when we feel powerless to control a situation or outcome. This helps explain why we live in what Dr. Robert Leahy calls "the age of anxiety."[2]

We live in a time and a culture in which people have never been more determined to be autonomous and yet at the same time, everything feels extremely uncertain. Thanks to the internet and real-time news notifications, we've never been more aware of just how vulnerable and powerless we

---

1. Edward M. Hallowell, "Managing Toxic Worry," adapted from *Worry: Hope and Help for a Common Condition* (New York: Ballentine, 1997), https://drhallowell .com/2018/01/31/managing-toxic-worry.
2. Robert L. Leahy, "The Age of Anxiety: Are We Born to Worry?" Heal Your Life, May 2, 2010, www.healyourlife.com/the-age-of-anxiety.

are. We instinctively know our way is never gonna work. It's not surprising that statistically there's never been a time in history when we've been more anxious than we are right here and right now. (This would be a natural place to give evidence of this by citing some statistics, but the dramatically increasing levels of anxiety mean that by the time you read the data, it will likely be irrelevant.)

Anxious in Many Ways

In the previous chapters, as we've been diagnosing our disconnection, we've looked at different Old Testament characters who found themselves in a place where their way wasn't working. These Old Testament stories show the need for a deeper connection and help us recognize the emotions that surface when we're living a disconnected life.

The emotion of anxiety alerts us to the reality that instead of connecting with God and depending on his power when we are vulnerable and powerless, we are making it about ourselves.

Do you remember the story of Moses and the burning bush in the book of Exodus? God is ready to send Moses on a mission to free his people from Egypt. As Moses hears this assignment, there's no doubt he is experiencing *heightened vulnerability* and *lack of control*.

His response to God reveals his anxiety. In Exodus 3:11, we read, "Moses said to God, 'Who am I that I should go to Pharaoh and bring the Israelites out of Egypt?'" This isn't false modesty from Moses. He is struggling with insecurity and the uncertainty of what is happening around him. Think through some reasons for Moses's anxiety:

He Had Already Tried and Failed

Moses is living in obscurity on the far side of the wilderness because he had to flee from Egypt. When Moses lived in Egypt as a younger man, he was upset when he saw the way his people were enslaved and abused. One day, he had seen an Egyptian beating one of his fellow Hebrews and decided to do something about it. He killed the Egyptian and buried the body in the sand.[3] Moses was forced to leave behind the life he knew and run for his life. He had tried things his way, and it didn't work.

It appears Moses resigned himself to a life of working for his father-in-law on the far side of the wilderness. It's not that he didn't want to help his people; it's just that he didn't know what to do. What he had done didn't help—in fact, it probably made things worse. What could he do now? The entire situation seemed out of his control.

He Was Worried about What People Would Think

This chapter began by asking a long series of "what if" questions, and that's the question Moses asks God. He asks God, in essence, *What if the Israelites want to know the name of the one who appointed me to confront Pharaoh and bring the people out*

---

3. The story is told in Exodus 2:11–22.

of Egypt? (see Exodus 3:13–15). Later on, Moses asks, "What if they do not believe me or listen to me and say, 'The LORD did not appear to you'?" (4:1). If we're honest, most of us would admit that what determines "my way" is what other people think.

Anxiety makes us self-focused. Quite a bit of research has been done about how the rise of social media has given way to an epidemic rise in anxiety. Why? It causes us to obsess about our lives, our image, and the way others perceive us. When the last thing on our minds when we fall asleep is what's on our Facebook feed, the Instagram photos we're not in, or the stories we've missed on Snapchat, we wake up in the middle of the night and can't sleep. So we start staring at the screen again.

He Doesn't Have What It Takes

In Exodus 4:10, you can hear the anxiety Moses feels as he imagines standing in front of Pharaoh and speaking to millions of his own people. Moses pleads to God, "O Lord, I'm not very good with words. I never have been, and I'm not now, even though you have spoken to me. I get tongue-tied, and my words get tangled" (NLT). Moses seems to think none of this honest self-appraisal has occurred to God. He's letting God in on some "new information." God's way doesn't make sense to him.

Notice that God doesn't address the anxiety that Moses is feeling by trying to convince him that he has what it takes. Instead, he reminds Moses that what's important is the connection he has with the one who gave him a tongue: "Then the LORD asked Moses, 'Who makes a person's mouth? Who decides whether people speak or do not speak, hear or do not hear, see or do not see? Is it not I, the LORD? Now go! I will be with you as you speak, and I will instruct you in what to say'" (Exodus 4:11–12 NLT).

We have a tendency, I think, to be hard on Moses, but think of the anxiety you feel when you sense God asking you to speak on his behalf to a neighbor, friend, or coworker. Most of us would argue that there must be a better way.

As I was growing up, I could never say my *r*'s. "Red rooster" sounded like "wed wooster." It's weally cute when you awe thwee or fouw, but when you awe in the fouwth gwade, it's not neawly as gweat. Okay, I'll stop, although pawt of me wants to do that for the west of the chaptew, just to dwive home the point.

As I got older, the problem didn't go away, and some of the kids in class began making fun of me. They would pull out their ears and say, "Wed wover, wed wover, send Kyle wight ovew." (Oh yeah, I had big ears too.) Adults wouldn't always understand me, and I'd have to repeat myself. I started going to speech therapy a few days a week and eventually began improving. But years later, I'd still feel anxious talking in front of a crowd, and I never thought I could be a pweacher.

The Task Seems Dangerous and Overwhelming

A few years ago, Amazon released an interesting piece of trivia. When people order an eBook, apparently Amazon can track which portions of the book a reader highlights. After accumulating seven years of data, Amazon revealed the most highlighted passage is a line from the second Hunger Games book. Here's the sentence that was highlighted more than any other: *Sometimes things happen to people and they're not equipped to deal with them.*

Can you imagine people reading the book and choosing to highlight that passage? A fifteen-year-old girl reads the book, but constantly checks her Instagram to see if her latest post has gained any more likes while she listens to her parents yelling in the other room. A man trying to pass the time in an addiction recovery center picks up the book to try to connect with his daughter, who hasn't talked to him in weeks. A wife who recently discovered texts between her husband and his mistress is reading this sentence in bed before falling asleep. A cancer patient reads it as they wait for their next treatment. It could be anyone, because everyone eventually experiences the reality that sometimes things happen that we are not equipped to deal with.

We become anxious when it becomes clear that life is going to be different from what we pictured. Maybe when Moses was a young man, he would have been up for the mission God was giving him. But now he has his life planned out. It wasn't necessarily exciting, but it was safe, and it was predictable. The older you get, the more "safe and predictable" tends to be the way you want it.

Not only was Moses living a fairly risk-free life, but he had also become quite reclusive. For the past forty years, he had spent the majority of his time tending sheep and living in the wilderness. Now he is asked to stand in front of the most powerful man in the world and to lead thousands of people.

Hear the fear and anxiety in his voice as Moses pleads with God: "Pardon your servant, Lord. Please send someone else" (Exodus 4:13).

God responds to all of these anxious objections of Moses, not by highlighting Moses's competency, but by emphasizing the connection God has to Moses: "But Moses said to God, 'Who am I that I should go to Pharaoh and bring the Israelites out of Egypt?' And God said, 'I will be with you'" (Exodus 3:11–12).

The answer to Moses's anxiety was not to affirm Moses's way but to assure Moses that God was with him. He just needed to remember and live in that connection. God's way always works.

Dealing with the Feeling

All of Moses's anxieties were focused on circumstances he couldn't control, problems he couldn't fix, and situations that were beyond his abilities. When our way isn't working and the emotion of anxiety starts to show up, we have different ways of dealing with it.

Like Moses, we sometimes run away and hide. It's the difference between the player on the bench who looks at the coach with an eagerness to get in the game and the player who stares at the gym floor to avoid eye contact because he's remembering the air ball he threw up the last time he was in the game.

One of the ways we run from our anxiety is to try to numb it with medications. Let me hasten to say that I know many of you have been diagnosed with an anxiety disorder for which medications are making a difference. I'm grateful for that. I'm proud of you for getting help. I'm certainly not criticizing you. But I am encouraging you to make sure that medicine isn't your first or even primary response to the anxiety you are feeling. Don't let a pill become a quick fix or cheap substitute for connecting with God's presence.

In his book *High Society*, Joseph Califano Jr., who at the time was the chairman of the National Center on Addiction and Substance Abuse at Columbia University, writes about this dynamic in our culture:

> Chemistry is chasing Christianity as the nation's largest religion. . . . Indeed, millions of Americans who in times of personal crisis and emotional and mental anguish once turned to priests, ministers, and rabbis for keys to the heavenly kingdom now go to physicians and psychiatrists, who hold the keys to the kingdom of pharmaceutical relief, or to drug dealers and liquor stores, as chemicals and alcohol replace the confessional as a source of solace and forgiveness.[4]

---

4. Joseph A. Califano Jr., *High Society: How Substance Abuse Ravages America and What to Do about It* (New York: PublicAffairs, 2007), 1–2.

Instead of considering whether the anxiety we feel is an indication that there could be something in our life that isn't working and needs attention, we sometimes take meds to help us ease that feeling.

I tend to run away from the anxiety of a moment, not by popping a pill, but by staring at a screen. If you're feeling anxious and scrolling mindlessly through social media or watching the latest YouTube video until you can't keep your eyes open anymore, perhaps this behavior is just a way to keep you from acknowledging that your way isn't working.

Control Issues

Maybe you deal with anxiety by going into control mode. If I asked you to tell me specifically what causes you anxiety, what isn't working in your life, what would you say? Chances are many of you wouldn't point to circumstances or mention a situation; rather, you'd tell me the name of a person. It's not that you can't control a situation; it's that you can't control a person.

You think your way would be working if that person would only do what he's supposed to do, if only she would feel the way you want her to feel, if only they would change the way they should have changed a long time ago. Maybe it's a friend with whom you shared some secrets. You trusted her enough to say some things to her that you've never said to anybody. And then one day, she starts hanging out with some other friends and stops replying to your texts and commenting on posts—for the most part she has ghosted you. Now you see the things your friend is doing with other friends, and it makes you feel anxious because you want to be included and you're not. You want to be in control, but what can you do?

Or maybe your anxiety has to do with a significant other in your life—a person you want to feel a certain way about you, to have feelings about you that they don't have. You want them to feel attracted to you, but their response is outside of your control. The more you try to control them, the more they push you away. The more they push you away, the more anxious you feel. The more anxious you feel, the more you try to control them. The more you try to control them, the more they push you away. The more they push you away, the more anxious you feel. The cycle of anxiety is off and running. And now you're just full of "what if" questions. *What if he never says it? What if she never feels that way? What if there's someone else?* There's so much in life we can't control.

Parents live out this dynamic continually. When it comes to our kids, we think, *If I can just control their decisions and their feelings and their choices and their entertainment and their friendships, everything will be fine.* We see them going down a path, and we think, *What if they can't come back from this experience? What if they can't turn things around? What if they marry the person they're dating? What if they never come back home? What if they never leave home?* We become anxious as it becomes clear that we can't control them.

But when we find ourselves in a position where we can't control what happens next, remember this: it's an invitation to a closer connection.

In 2 Corinthians 1, Paul reveals some of the anxiety he's feeling. He lists some things he's going through that are beyond his control—situations in which he knows his way isn't going to work: "We were crushed and overwhelmed beyond our ability to endure, and we thought we would never live through it. In fact, we expected to die" (2 Corinthians 1:8–9 NLT). But then he gives us the answer to the question of why he and his companions faced such adversity: "This happened that we might not rely on ourselves but on God, who raises the dead" (1:9). The anxiety he was dealing with gave him the opportunity to connect with the presence and power of God in a way he had never experienced.

Moses also testified to this result. While he resisted God's mission initially out of fear and anxiety, he learned that his connection with God was ultimately the only thing that mattered. Fast-forward to what must have been one of the most anxious moments of Moses's life. Moses has led the people out of Egypt and is heading toward the promised land. They seem to be making good progress, but then they reach a place where the way they've been going stops working. They come to the Red Sea and are no longer able to move forward. With Pharaoh's armies closing in behind them, there's nowhere left to turn.

The people Moses is leading begin to panic and blame him. So Moses stands in front of the people and says, "The

LORD will fight for you; you need only to be still" (Exodus 14:14). If he is feeling anxious, he doesn't show it. His confidence is in his connection with God.

When your way isn't working and you're facing an uncertain future, a situation you can't control, be still and let God fight for you.

THE WAY OF CONNECTION

I am the vine; you are the branches.

—JESUS

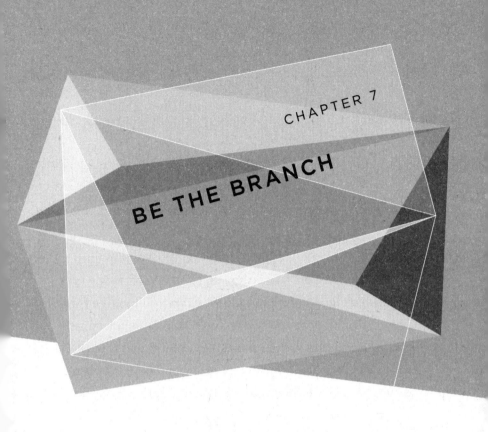

CHAPTER 7

BE THE BRANCH

In the spring of 2021, a video of a valedictorian speech given by a graduating high school senior named Kyle Martin went viral. In his speech, Martin talked about the moment he realized he was in the running for valedictorian. The amount of work he had put in and the sacrifices he had made to receive this honor were huge. As he talked about the time and effort required to earn the highest GPA in the class, the assumption was that he was leading to a moment when he would make the point that all his hard work had paid off and it was all worth it in the end. Martin shared the moment he found out he had won the valedictorian title:

It's so good, for about 15 seconds. Yeah, 15 seconds of my heart racing and my adrenaline pumping. 15 seconds of "Yeah I won!" 15 seconds of being at the top of the pile of all my accomplishments and it felt euphoric. But there must come a 16th second. And on that 16th second, I sat down on my seat, I looked at my silver stole that says valedictorian, and I thought, "That's it? What just happened? Why am I not feeling anything else?"

Martin went on: "To be honest, I don't even know what I was expecting. A parade of balloons to drop? Or maybe I was hoping that all of my problems would fade away in comparison to this amazing achievement. But none of that happened, not even in my heart. I felt nothing. I was shocked. This was a huge problem for me, and I needed to figure out why."[1]

Kyle Martin was discovering something that high achievers are often slow to realize—namely, that if your way is to put in the work and sacrifice whatever must be sacrificed in order to be successful, everyone around you may celebrate your accomplishments and treat you as though your way is working . . . and then comes the sixteenth second.

Connection over Production

John 15 contains some of Jesus' final words to his closest followers. Jesus knows that later in the evening, he will be

---

1. Laurie Pitts, "Kyle Martin Regrets Finishing Top of His Class and It Makes for the Best Valedictorian Speech," GodUpdates, January 29, 2020, www.godupdates.com/kyle-martin-best-valedictorian-speech.

arrested in Gethsemane. Jesus will soon be leaving his disciples with a mission to take the good news to the ends of the earth. It's difficult to overstate the magnitude of that assignment. The task ahead will require incredible work and sacrifice.

You may think that with his final words, Jesus will give them a five-year plan that lays out the expectations and outlines the pace of productivity required to have maximum impact. Perhaps you expect him to hand out a task list along with a comprehensive strategy for success, or maybe provide a series of charts that plot out the actionable items that need attention. At the very least, you assume Jesus will print out some sort of organizational chart that will give official job descriptions and best practices.

Yet instead of focusing on production, Jesus prioritizes connection. Jesus knew that if his followers would focus on staying connected with him, then production would come, but if they pursued production at the expense of connection, then it wouldn't matter how hard they worked. Jesus put it this way in John 15:4–5:

> Remain in me, as I also remain in you. No branch can bear fruit by itself; it must remain in the vine. Neither can you bear fruit unless you remain in me.
>
> I am the vine; you are the branches. If you remain in me and I in you, you will bear much fruit; apart from me you can do nothing.

Over the years, I've heard a number of messages on this

text that emphasize fruit bearing. The priority is on production. When your way isn't working, you need to produce more fruit. The application goes something like this: *It's time to examine your life and look for the fruit. If there isn't enough fruit, it's time to buckle down and get to work. You don't want to be a stick with no fruit that gets thrown into the fires of hell, so you better set your alarm, rise, and grind. It's time to hustle harder!*

This is not at all what Jesus is saying; in fact, it's a dangerous misinterpretation of his words. It's not that fruitfulness doesn't matter; it's that we can't make it happen on our own. If you make production your primary priority, Jesus makes it clear that your way isn't going to work. It's all about *connection*.

The challenge for most of us is that when our way isn't working, our default is to double down on production. Our instinct is to start working harder to try to make things happen. The equation that makes the most sense is this: greater effort leads to greater production. But when that strategy doesn't seem to help, we become discouraged, frustrated, anxious, and burned-out. What Jesus wants his disciples (you and me) to never forget is that everything begins with connection. The focus is on connection over production. The priority is on abiding over achieving.

Reasons We Prioritize Production over Connection

Why do we prioritize production over connection? There are a number of reasons, and I'll suggest a few here.

Approval Points

It's engrained in us from the time we are young that results get rewarded. The last time I went to a fifth-grade graduation, I noticed all the awards that were given for production and performance: Top Reader, Science Star, Times Table Titan, Spelling Bee Champion, Cursive King and Queen, and Writing Wizard. While it's certainly appropriate to recognize and reward hard work and achievement, it shouldn't be surprising we've become wired to prioritize production over connection. It's production that gets us praise, promotions, and pay raises.

Some people grew up in homes in which connection was dependent on production. The not-so-subtle message was that affection and approval were based on accomplishments. If you brought home straight As, you'd get lots of affirmation, but if you brought home a C or two, then you could expect some criticism. If you scored enough points in the game, your dad would be proud of you, pat you on the back, and take you out for ice cream, but if you rode the bench, he would be disappointed—and that felt like disconnection.

This message certainly gets reinforced in the church. I remember going to church camp as a kid and hoping to win "Camper of the Week." A camper won the award by doing things like memorizing the most Bible verses, praying out loud in a group, and cleaning up in the cafeteria after meals. Again, I am all for acknowledging hard work and creative ways to teach important habits, but the not-so-subtle message was that the camper of the week was the one who was best at production.

It's not just that we prioritize production over connection; it's that we think production is a prerequisite for connection. We think that connection with God or others has to be earned. We subconsciously approach our relationship with God this way, thinking that the best way to connect with him is through producing for him. And so we live our lives under this crushing burden, believing we need to produce more in order to earn God's acceptance and approval. We think of our good deeds as chips we can cash in for connection.

God doesn't withhold relationship from us until we produce enough to earn it. Your church attendance, volunteer hours, generosity, and acts of compassion are not the currency that pays for God's affection. God's way is exactly the opposite. Production flows best out of connection. We think that production will lead to connection, but Jesus makes it clear: connection leads to production.

As a pastor, I have conversations with people who have visited church a few times. They often have questions about what they need to do to become a Christian. They instinctively say things like, "Well, when I get my life turned around"; "If I could just get clean and stay clean for a couple weeks"; "When I get out of this relationship"; "When I stop having such an anger problem"—maybe then I'll start going to church and become a Christian. In other words, "Let me start producing, and then Jesus will let me connect."

In John 15, Jesus makes it clear it's not production that leads to connection. We can experience incredible freedom and motivation when we get this right. It's connection that empowers production in our lives.

The B. S. Factor

B. S. stands for "bootstraps," as you probably guessed, which is used in the phrase "pulling yourself up by your own bootstraps." *Bootstrapping* refers to the ability to get ourselves out of a difficult situation or to make something happen without requiring external help or input. It appeals to our pride and ego. Being the branch implies a level of dependence and insufficiency that we are reluctant to admit to.

The bootstraps factor is the feeling of self-sufficiency that comes when we make something happen despite difficult circumstances. Connection means we require help and strength from another source and can't make things happen on our own.

I recently helped one of our daughters prepare for a job interview by talking through some commonly asked questions she could expect. I told her that the person interviewing her would likely ask her some variation of the question, "What is your greatest weakness?" I foolishly explained that she shouldn't point to her greatest weakness; instead, she needed to think about a weakness she had overcome and turned into a strength. Something like, "Well, I can sometimes be so driven to complete a task that I overlook parts of my personal life, but I've learned to set better boundaries and to live a more balanced life without sacrificing productivity." In other words, *I'm so capable that even one of my great weaknesses is actually further evidence of how strong I am.*

The truth is, the moment I admit weakness and ask for help, I can no longer wear the "DIY badge" with pride. Instead of being the person who made it happen, I'm the person who needed help to make it happen. Prioritizing connection over production is difficult for a bootstrapper who can't accept their own weakness or recognize that the do-it-yourself way of living isn't working.

Compensating for Feelings of Failure

By being hyperfocused on production in one area of life, I can feel better about my failures in another area. I've had seasons as a husband and father when I felt like I wasn't getting the job done and didn't know what to do. In those seasons, my problem wasn't a lack of effort. Despite giving my best, it became clear that my way just wasn't working. I wasn't seeing the fruit I knew should be there.

Instead of "being the branch" and working on my connection with Jesus and others to find the strength and help I need, my tendency is to turn my attention to a part of my life where I can better control the outcome and produce the results. So I start spending longer hours at work or more time in the gym. If I'm producing in these other areas in ways that get noticed and appreciated, I don't have to think about another area where I'm coming up short. If I don't know what to do about a certain situation, I just focus on what I do know instead of admitting my weakness and inability to do it on my own.

Measuring Up

Connection is difficult to measure, but production can usually be tracked, calculated, and assessed. We like to be able to point to what we produce and measure our results.

Here's an example of how this plays out for me: I come home after a long day at work and I'm thinking about what my evening is going to look like. The grass really needs to be mowed, or I could go for a walk with my wife. I would certainly enjoy walking with my wife more than cutting the grass. I know doing something together would mean a lot to her, and we've agreed that we need to spend more time connecting by doing things like going on evening walks.

Even though I would prefer to go for a walk, I'm more likely to end up mowing the lawn. Why? Because when I'm done mowing, I have something to show for it. I can point to my freshly mowed yard and say, "Look what I did." If I go for a walk with my wife, the signs of my productivity aren't nearly as tangible. When the walk is over, it feels like we end up in the same place where we started without much to show for it. Connection is difficult to measure, so I'll usually default to production.

A few years ago, I baptized an older woman who had attended church for a while but had put off making a decision to express her belief in Jesus and follow him. When I met her backstage, she introduced herself and then immediately told me she had been baptized as a baby, never missed

SECTION 2: THE WAY OF CONNECTION

church as a child, and has been attending here for years. She keeps on her nightstand a special Bible given to her by her grandmother. She loves to listen to sermons and take notes— she has filled several notebooks. She serves in a ministry that collects winter coats for people in need.

I finally cut her off with these words. "I'm sorry, but none of that is enough." I said it gently and with a smile to let her know I was making a point. She was still caught off guard. I don't think she realized what she was doing. But like many of us, she was approaching her relationship with Jesus like it was an application to a college she was hoping to get into. I proceeded to encourage her in what she was doing, but I wanted to make it clear that Jesus didn't want a relationship with her because he wanted more and more *from* her. He simply wanted more and more *of* her—and more and more of you as well. As you connect with him, the production will come.

Production versus Connection

The gospel of Luke includes a story that shows what it looks like when we prioritize connection over production—it's a picture of what it means to "be the branch." Luke tells of two sisters, one who was prioritizing production and the other who was absorbed in connection.

Mary and Martha and their brother, Lazarus, were friends of Jesus. They lived a few miles outside of Jerusalem in the town of Bethany. One day, Jesus stopped by to see

116

them. Luke 10:38 tells us, "As Jesus and his disciples were on their way, he came to a village where a woman named Martha opened her home to him."

We aren't sure how many people were traveling with Jesus at the time, but there were at least the twelve disciples. Having more than a dozen hungry people show up at their house unannounced meant a lot of things needed to happen quickly. Martha, who seems to be the older of the two sisters, immediately felt the stress of having to get things cleaned up and food prepared for her guests.

Luke 10:39 tells us that Martha's sister Mary "sat at the Lord's feet listening to what he said." Don't miss this: she was sitting at Jesus' feet. This wasn't something that would have been culturally acceptable for a woman to do. Sitting at the feet of a rabbi was a position reserved for men. But Mary takes the posture of a chosen disciple and sits at his feet listening. The next verse continues: "But Martha was distracted by all the preparations that had to be made."

There are two sisters. Mary prioritizes connection with Jesus; Martha is preoccupied with production. Martha was distracted by all the prep work that had to be done. While we may be tempted to criticize her for not joining Mary and sitting at the feet of Jesus, it's not like she was in the other room scrolling through Instagram or shopping on Amazon. She was being hospitable and working to make sure Jesus and his disciples were taken care of. The pull of production over connection often feels like "being responsible."

A few years ago, one of my daughters was working as a

delivery driver for Door Dash. She picked up food from restaurants and delivered the food to customers. One evening it was pouring rain. I didn't like the idea of her making deliveries in the stormy weather, so I asked if I could tag along. We stopped at the first restaurant, and since it was raining, I volunteered to go in and get the food.

I walked into the restaurant where a woman was standing behind the counter. I said, "Hey, I'm the delivery driver, and I'm here to pick up food for delivery to a customer."

She got excited and said, "You're my pastor!" Before I had a chance to jump in and explain that I was helping my daughter, she added, "I always wondered what pastors did when it wasn't Sunday."

I started to defend myself. For some reason it bothered me that she didn't understand how much work I really do. So I started to give a lengthy explanation of how demanding my job is. Halfway into my rant, I laughed at myself for feeling like I needed to make it clear that I was helping my daughter and for trying to defend how important my pastoral position is. Too often, I attach my identity and worth to my position. I take too much pride in my production and the outward appearance—the things other people see.

Picture Martha in the other room, feeling good about herself but getting more and more annoyed with Mary. Martha feels compelled to do all the work. It's not that Martha wouldn't rather be sitting in the room listening to Jesus, but there are things that need to be done. I imagine her trying to get Mary's attention, giving Mary the look only a big sister can give that silently sends the message to Mary that she had better get off the floor and start helping.

Martha has finally had enough. She seems a bit annoyed that Jesus hasn't set her little sister straight. Luke 10:40 goes on to say, "She came to him and asked, 'Lord, don't you care that my sister has left me to do the work by myself? Tell her to help me!'"

Martha assumes Jesus will be on her side. Of course doing *something* has to be more spiritual than doing *nothing*. She is resentful that she's doing all the work while Mary is just sitting there listening.

Luke 10:41–42 tells us how Jesus responded: "Martha, Martha, . . . you are worried and upset about many things, but few things are needed—or indeed only one. Mary has chosen what is better, and it will not be taken away from her."

The Urgent versus the Important

Connection always feels like it can wait, but production feels like it needs to happen right now. I'm sure Martha told herself that when all the prep work was done, she would go in and spend time with Jesus. Maybe she reasoned to herself that the next time he was in town, she'd try to connect, but for now she had too many responsibilities to carry out.

Connection often feels like something we can catch up

on when things aren't so busy. We are going to start being more intentional to sit at the feet of Jesus, but now's just not a good time. And when we do try to spend some time connecting with him, we feel the pressure of what needs to be taken care of right away.

I start with my prayer list but end up thinking about my to-do list. One Sunday, during the passing of the elements at the Lord's Supper, I began to pray. It went something like this:

> *Jesus, thank you for the great sacrifice you made so that I could be forgiven. You made a way for me to be connected with you when there was nothing I could say and nothing I could offer. Nothing is more important to me than being deeply connected with you. I'm sorry for missing some of our time together this week.*

There was something about the word *missing* that made me think of missing trash day that week. My head was still bowed, but now here's what I'm thinking:

> I don't understand why the people who pick up trash can't come at a more consistent time. I know I had the trash cans out to the curb early enough. Next week, I'll set them out the night before. I wonder if that bill didn't get paid for some reason. Maybe I need to update my payment method. I know it's about time to update my driver's license. I need to make that appointment

before I forget. I guess I can do that on Wednesday, but Wednesday is my study day and I'd hate to get behind on my sermon about overcoming distractions.

I may start off with a desire for connection, but the urgency of production feels pressing. In reality, our connections are more urgent than we realize. Martha couldn't have known how little time Jesus had left on earth and how limited her opportunities were to connect with him.

Our connections are more urgent than we realize. That's true when it comes to connecting with the significant people in our lives, but it's even more true when it comes to connecting with God. Psalm 39 records a prayer we would do well to pray every day: "LORD, remind me how brief my time on earth will be" (Psalm 39:4 NLT).

The Doing versus the Being

I recently served with another pastor from our church—a good friend of mine—at one of the food pantries supported by our church. When we got there, I noticed a number of pallets stacked with boxes of food that needed to be organized and stocked on the shelves. A few other volunteers were already hard at work, so I jumped in. Fifteen minutes into it, I was making some progress, but I was getting frustrated with my friend because he was nowhere to be seen. I stepped away to look for him and found him sitting at a table with a homeless man, visiting with him as he ate his lunch.

Want to guess my response? I was annoyed. There was work to be done and he was sitting there talking to someone he had just met—and would likely never see again. When it was time to leave, I looked at the shelves that were organized and stocked with food and was glad one of us had gotten something done instead of just "wasting time" talking with people. The fact that I was valuing production over connection was evident not just by what I prioritized but also by the way I was judging someone who didn't. It also points to the sad truth that, without even thinking about it, I value people by their doing—or lack of doing.

It's not that doing doesn't matter; it's that doing should flow from being. Being the branch, abiding in Christ, often doesn't feel like we're doing anything. But being connected always leads to fruitfulness in the most important ways.

Martha prioritizes doing, but Mary sits at the feet of Jesus and is commended for simply "being." The late Henri Nouwen wrote about living in a home with people who had significant disabilities. His time with them helped him realize that, more than he wanted to admit, he was still finding his identity and worth in doing rather than being:

Living with . . . [disabled] people, I realize how success-oriented I am. Living with men and women who cannot compete in the worlds of business, industry, sports, or academics, but for whom dressing, walking, speaking, eating, drinking, and playing are the main "accomplishments," is extremely frustrating for me. I may have come to the theoretical insight that being is more important than doing, but when asked to just be with people who can do very little I realize how far I am from the realization of that insight.[2]

I have a friend who likes to remind me, "God would love you just as much as he does right now if you decided to buy a house out in the country and spend the rest of your life on the front porch drinking lemonade." Theologically I know he's right. The Bible says, "While we were still sinners, Christ died for us" (Romans 5:8). The moment we were at our worst and most disconnected, God loved us so much that he "did not spare his own Son, but gave him up for us all" (Romans 8:32). But even though I technically agree with my friend, there's a part of me that resists this idea. I find myself wanting to attach God's love for me to my doing. I know biblically my inclination is wrong, but intuitively I get caught up trying to earn my connection with him.

One of the ways to check your "doing versus being" is to pay attention to the way you plan your calendar. Do you organize your time around production or connection? Do you plan your days around responsibilities or relationships? Clearly, God does not want us to neglect our responsibilities or ignore our duties. He wants us to be good stewards of what he has entrusted to us. The challenge to us in this chapter is to prioritize our connections—first with Jesus and

---

2. Henri J. M. Nouwen, *Lifesigns: Intimacy, Fecundity, and Ecstasy in Christian Perspective* (New York: Image, 1986), 51.

then with others—and then allow what our lives produce to flow from those connections.

Look at your calendar and schedule connective relationships and leave the leftover time for your productive responsibilities. I know this approach isn't always practical and unexpected things can pop up that make it seem impossible. But this commitment is worth fighting for, and it won't happen unless you intentionally work at it.

The Temporary versus the Eternal

In the moments of everyday living, production can feel pressing, but it's our connections that last forever. Think about the executive who recently retired and is struggling to make sense of why the company he poured his heart and soul into has forgotten about him. For decades he prioritized his work. He'd try to attend church with his family on Sundays, but that was his catch-up day. He was regularly invited to a men's Bible study on Thursday mornings, but that invitation conflicted with his goal of being the first one in the office. When he went on vacation with his family, he spent half the time on the phone working on a deal or in a Zoom meeting to make sure he didn't miss anything. When his kids were young, he tried to be home in time for family dinners, but his family usually had to start without him. He gave so much of his time to the company, but when he retired, they threw him a party, gave him a watch, and moved on without him.

Production is temporary, but connections are eternal.

Jesus says to Martha, "Mary has chosen what is better, and it will not be taken away from her" (Luke 10:42). The phrase *will not be taken away* sounds like Jesus is saying he won't tell Mary to help in the kitchen. That may be part of what Jesus is implying, but another way to understand this phrase is that what Mary is doing will *never* be taken from her because it will last forever. Mary has chosen what is better because what she has chosen is eternal.

In Kyle Martin's valedictorian speech, he talked about how that accomplishment felt great for about fifteen seconds. But in the sixteenth second, he started to realize that this great honor was paid for by sacrificing connection with the most important people in his life. Kyle put it this way:

> Working hard is good. It is in fact biblical. But it should not be done for the sole purpose of a goal's sake at the expense of relationship with others. Looking back on this year, I realized that the stress of this year, for this goal and a five-minute speech, was paid for with the lack of attending to relationships in my life. . . . Nothing is more important than your healthy relationships. Nothing. Not your goals, not your successes. . . . As you live your life on this earth, there is no greater good you can do for a person than to love them so much, that you point them to Jesus Christ. But first, he should be your first relationship that you cannot neglect.[3]

---

3. Pitts, "Kyle Martin Regrets."

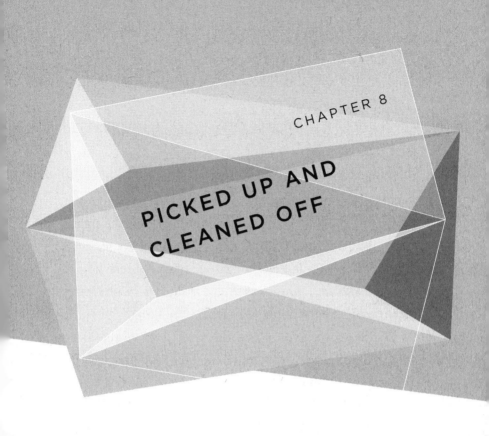

CHAPTER 8

PICKED UP AND CLEANED OFF

The question is, 'What would you do?' Good evening, I'm John Quiñones."

If you've ever watched the ABC hidden camera show called *What Would You Do?* when you read the first line of this chapter, you probably imitated John Quiñones's voice. If you didn't, I'll give you a second to try it. Make sure you emphasize the word *you*. What would *you* do?

If you were to ever hear those words in real life, you'd probably look for cameras and start sweating nervously while replaying in your head everything you said and did during the previous few minutes. If you've never seen or heard of the show—or been a part of it unwittingly—I'll give you a quick rundown.

The show serves as a social experiment of sorts. The producers plant a few trained actors in a public environment in which they are surrounded by ordinary, unsuspecting members of the community. With the prompting of the producers, the actors create a situation that tests the moral and ethical convictions of the people watching the scenario unfold. Here are a few of the episode titles: "Parent Leaves Baby in Hot Car," "Customer Abuses Employee with Down Syndrome," and "Muslim Teen Bullied by Peers."

As the viewer, you watch the actors initiate the awkward, inappropriate, or dangerous dilemma. You eagerly anticipate the response of the unknowing citizens. *Will they walk by with their heads down and ignore the issue? Will they join in on the inappropriate behavior? Will they stand up for what's right?* It's a fascinating concept because you get to witness the natural response of regular people in uncomfortable and challenging situations.

When our kids were younger, I would often watch that show with them. Before discovering how the people on the show responded, I would push pause and ask them, "What would *you* do?" It would provoke some internal reflection and interesting conversations. For the most part, we would all agree on the right thing to do, but we'd have a harder time agreeing on how to do the right thing. One of my kids would get emotionally invested. It may have been a hypothetical situation, but she was, for real, upset. What would *she* do? She would make a scene. Another daughter would talk about the best way to de-escalate the situation without drawing too much attention to the people involved.

The show allowed our family to question how we would respond if something was amiss in our own environment. If you witnessed some questionable behavior or a suspicious situation, would *you* speak up? Would *you* ignore it? What type of person are *you*?

Admittedly, it's hard to objectively answer this question from the comfort of our La-Z-Boy while eating dry Cinnamon Toast Crunch right out of the box,[1] but it's important to regularly wrestle with the question, "What would *you* do?"

We don't often stop and consider things from someone else's perspective. We don't often ask the question, "What would you do?" and even more rarely do we do that with God. But that's what I want to ask you to do as you read this chapter. Specifically, if you were God, what would *you* do about *you*?

Isaiah 55 states clearly that God's thoughts are not our thoughts and his ways are not our ways. We don't know what God knows. We can't see what he sees and don't sit where he sits. But take a moment to look at your life and consider what you would do with you if you were God. If

---

1. The way God intended it. My friend eats it with almond milk. As if the healthy choice of almond milk offsets the nutritional impact of the Cinnamon Toast Crunch. It doesn't. And besides, what is almond milk? Because you can't milk almonds, Greg.

you were God, completely perfect and all-powerful, what would you do with you?

> When you complain and act entitled, what would you do with you?
>
> When you keep doing what you know is wrong and not doing what you know is right, what would you do with you?
>
> When you keep missing opportunities to make a difference, what would you do with you?
>
> When you ignore God and are always too busy to spend time with him, what would you do with you?

It's natural to assume that when our way—which we insist on continuing—isn't working and things in our lives are a mess, God will cut us off and move on. It seems likely that he'll disconnect from us and leave us behind.

One way to get a more objective answer to that question is to look at the way you've dealt with people in your life who have disappointed you in some way. *Disappointed* may not be a strong enough term. How about abandoned? Rejected? Betrayed? Ignored? Ghosted? Neglected? Deserted? Chances are this isn't a hypothetical, "what if" kind of exercise.

We've all experienced deep disappointment on some level. Depending on the severity and frequency, we usually reach a point where cutting the person off and having nothing to do with them seems like the way to go. They didn't come through for us, and so we will no longer have anything to do with them. Most of us have more than a few people we have cut off. You don't have to defend yourself. I get it—they had it coming.

A lot of us have stepped away, and people have walked away from us as well. There is the friend you ghosted because she always needed something from you. The coworker you quit talking to because you're pretty sure they started the rumor about you. The ex whose name you don't speak. The sibling you haven't contacted for years. The child who has stopped speaking to you. The neighbor you avoid. When it becomes hard to keep track of all the disconnections and you look back to see in your wake a group of people who have been left behind, it becomes clearer what you would do with you if you were God.

I have on my phone a list of "blocked contacts." When anyone in my family who is on my iCloud account blocks a number, it gets put on this list. I was surprised by how many numbers were on it. I'm sure most of them were numbers of telemarketers who kept calling and wanting to sell something. The list contained at least two numbers of boys who were interested in one of my daughters when she was younger—and of course I didn't want their texts or calls going through to her.[2] There's the number of an extended family member who wasn't respecting boundaries. There's the number of a plumber who lied to us and cheated us out of money. There were several numbers with names I

---

2. Only dads who've had teenage daughters are allowed to judge me.

recognized, but I'm not sure of the story that resulted in them getting blocked. Those phone numbers answer the question about what we do, at least eventually, when someone hurts us, takes advantage of us, or constantly wants something from us: they get blocked.

In John 15, as Jesus walks with his disciples, he references the vine and branches. He has explained to his closest followers that he is the *Vine*, we are the *branches*, and God is the *Gardener*. He talks to them about how the Gardener deals with disappointing branches that have stopped bearing fruit. These are the branches that can't be relied on. Branches that look promising but never seem to produce. Branches that are always saying that things will change but they never do. What does God the Gardener do with such branches? Does he ghost you? Does he cut you off? Does he block you? When your way isn't working—and it's all your fault—does he disconnect from you?

The answer to those questions invites you to a deeper connection with the Vine and calls you to reconnect with some people you've cut off.

God the Gardener

Throughout John 15, we read about the way in which God deals with three different kinds of branches. First, we read about what God does with unproductive branches, and if truth be told, it sounds a little harsh: "He cuts off every branch in me that bears no fruit" (John 15:2).

Hmm . . . well, that doesn't sound encouraging. That sounds like if we aren't good enough, if we don't produce enough, God cuts us off. He moves on without us. If what that sounds like is what actually happens, then none of us stand a chance at experiencing a life of connection with the Vine.

But if the Gardener simply cuts off every branch that bears no fruit, then it seems contradictory to what Jesus will go on to teach about the vine and the branches. Jesus promises that if we remain in him and stay connected with him, we will bear fruit (John 15:5). So how can Jesus say that God "cuts off every branch in me that bears no fruit"? He seems to suggest that it's possible to be connected with the vine without bearing fruit and that if you're not bearing fruit, God has no use for you.

Maybe that sounds right to you, especially if you grew up in a church that was all about performance. When I was a kid in Sunday school, a chart hung on the wall. A column on the far left of the chart contained all the names of the Sunday school regular attenders. Across the top was a list of things you could do to earn a gold star sticker.

Here is the list of some of things that earn you a gold star: coming to church, bringing your Bible, memorizing the weekly Bible verse, bringing an offering, inviting a friend to come with you, and volunteering to pray. Oh, and there were a few other ways to earn a gold star: having good manners, sitting still during the lesson, having your shirt tucked in, and helping pick up the classroom. So every week you could look at your name on the chart and see how many gold stars you had lined up.

After a couple of months, the chart contained some names that had dozens of gold stars and some that had one or two. At the end of the year, the Sunday school teacher brought doughnuts and chocolate milk and threw a party for all the kids with a certain number of stars. And even though it was never said out loud, it was obvious to all of us kids which ones of us were God's favorites and which ones he was disappointed in.

Is that how our relationship with God works? Does he cut off everyone who hasn't earned a certain number of gold stars? Does he tolerate us as long as our production numbers are up and to the right, but if we begin to wither and don't bear enough fruit, he "cuts us off"?

Cut Off or Picked Up

In Greek, the word for "cut off" is *airo*. It is a relatively common word in the New Testament, and it generally means something along the lines of "remove" or "lift up." So it's reasonable to conclude, as the NIV does, that Jesus is talking about a gardener cutting off or "removing" the dying branches. If that's an accurate translation, then perhaps it's because God as Gardener is removing branches that have died but have yet to fall from the vine—like cutting down a tree that is dead but hasn't yet fallen.

At the same time, an equally valid translation is that God

PICKED UP AND CLEANED OFF

"picks up" or "lifts up" the dying branches. The word *airo* appears twenty-six times in the gospel of John. Check out how it's used in John 5:8, where Jesus says to a paralyzed man, "*Pick up* your mat and walk." We see it again in John 8:59 where the religious leaders, who are furious with Jesus, "*picked up* stones to stone him." Yes, it can refer to taking something away, but it can also refer to picking something up. So Jesus might be saying that God the Gardener "cuts off" dead branches, but he might also be saying that God "picks up" dying branches. Those are vastly different interpretations with two very different implications.

Imagine you're the parent of a teen girl who just got her driver's license. You're continually reminding her of the importance of taking good care of her vehicle: "Make sure you remember to fill your car with gas." "Remember to get your oil changed." Despite your reminders, she is pretty careless, cruising around without paying much attention to the fuel gauge. You know it's just a matter of time until she runs out of gas. You're also confident that when she runs out of gas, it will be just as much your problem as it is hers.

One day, you get a phone call from your daughter. When you answer the phone, she confesses, "I've run out of gas." Her voice is sort of muffled by the sound of other cars on the freeway zipping by her. She's having a hard time hearing you, so you hang up and send her a text: "I'm going to *airo* you." What does *that* mean? Well, it could mean, "I'm going to *pick you up*." But it could also mean, "I'm going to *cut you off*."

For your teen daughter, the meaning of *airo* is of grave importance. If it means, "I'm going to pick you up," your daughter is relieved. Help is on the way. If it means, "I'm going to cut you off," then your daughter is distraught. She is on her own. You warned her this would happen, and she's getting what she deserves. When her way isn't working, is she picked up or cut off?

As she sits on the side of the road with a combination of shame for running out of gas and fear as cars speed by, she reads the text again: "I'm going to *airo* you." Her interpretation of that word—"pick up" or "cut off"—is largely determined by the experiences she has had with her father over the years. Her interpretation is clarified by her father's character.

The definition of *airo* is a small detail with huge implications. How we understand and define *airo* will determine how we connect with God when our way isn't working. When we become too much trouble or are too high-maintenance, when we ignore what he has clearly said and disobey what he has told us, when we wither and struggle to produce good fruit, is God the kind of gardener who picks us up or cuts us off?

Many of us have lived lives of disconnection and have been resistant to seek reconnection with Jesus because we have a "cut you off" theology. We know what we have done and what we haven't done. We know a lot of gold stars are missing from our chart in heaven. If we were God, we know deep down what we would do with us. And so we assume rejection and keep our distance.

Several years ago, I was at a conference with a few hundred church leaders from around the country. I was excited to see an old friend. I hadn't seen him in a few years, but we used to be close. When I went over to give him a hug, he didn't return the embrace. He just kind of stood there. It was awkward. After a few minutes of forced small talk, we went our separate ways. I wasn't sure what was going on, but it was obvious he had a problem with me.

Later that day, I asked him if he wanted to get breakfast with me in the morning. He looked at me a little confused but reluctantly agreed. When we sat down at the breakfast table, I said to him, "Hey, I might have misread things, but yesterday when we talked, it seemed like something was wrong. I know we haven't connected in a while. I just want to make sure things are good with us."

Without saying a word, he took out his phone and clicked on his message app. He entered something in the search space and then handed me his phone. I read through a half dozen text messages he had sent to me—ones I had never replied to. His last text message read, "Okay, you seem to be ignoring me. I won't bother you anymore." I was confused because I hadn't heard from him in years and I knew I hadn't blocked his number, but I had never seen his messages.

Suddenly I realized what had happened. I checked the number he had been using—and sure enough, he had been texting my old number. For the past several years, he thought I had ghosted him. When he thought he had been cut off, what was his response? He decided to quit trying. He thought I had removed him from my life, so he disconnected and walked away.

I wonder how often we've disconnected with God in that way. We wrongly think we've been cut off and that he's done with us. We feel rejected and discarded, so we stop coming to church and we give up on praying. What's the point if God isn't going to respond to our messages? We assume we did something wrong or maybe we just didn't earn enough gold stars, but we convince ourselves that we've been cut off.

The Bible makes it clear. God is "slow to anger, abounding in love and faithfulness" (Exodus 34:6; Psalm 103:8) and will never leave us nor forsake us (Deuteronomy 31:6; Hebrews 13:5). But when we think about what we have done or have not done, we tend to assume that God is a vengeful gardener with a machete in hand, ready to lop off any branch that isn't producing enough fruit. We try to be good enough to keep God from snapping, but we're not sure what the standard for "good enough" is. Thus we spend our lives oscillating between self-righteousness (because we think we've met the standard) and shame (because we're certain that we've fallen short).

I truly believe that God loves me, forgives me, and has saved me from my sin. I know that those things are true, but if I'm honest, I sometimes feel that God is frustrated with me. I feel like he barely tolerates me and if I don't start producing some serious fruit, he's going to cut me off.

You've felt that too? This subtle but malignant misunderstanding of God probably stems from a different place for every person.

It could be your hometown preacher who shouted about God's truth and whispered about God's grace.

It could be your ex who snuck out of the picture as soon as your personality became problematic, leaving you to feel as though loving you is a burden that no one is able to carry.

It could be that when you ran out of gas on the side of the road, you knew you had better not call your dad because when he shows up, he's going to be furious.

It could be the series of tragedies that plagued your life, causing you to question whether God was punishing you for not being good enough.

Ultimately, the real source of this is an enemy who wants to convince you that you have been ghosted by God and that he is going to cut you off.

Pick You Up

Which is it? *Cut off* or *picked up*?

One of my favorites passages of Scripture is Romans 8:38–39. Here the apostle Paul pushes back against the feeling that God has rejected us:

> For I am convinced that neither death nor life, neither
> angels nor demons, neither the present nor the future, nor
> any powers, neither height nor depth, nor anything else
> in all creation, will be able to separate us from the love of
> God that is in Christ Jesus our Lord.

I am not sure if Paul could state any more clearly that the love of God for us is unchangeable. Nothing can alter it. Not your wasted time, not your apathetic indifference, not your passive disobedience, not your divorce, not your addiction, not your affair, not your procrastination, not your bad habits, not your short temper, not your harsh words, not your biggest regret, not your blank gold-star-sticker chart—nothing can separate you from the love of God that is in Christ Jesus our Lord.

The definition of *airo* became even clearer to me when I spent some time one day walking with the owner of a local vineyard. I asked him questions about how he cared for the branches. Listening to him, and more importantly watching him, gave me a clearer picture of God as the gardener.

He sees a branch that is connected with the vine but has no fruit on it. This branch is in the dirt, surrounded by weeds that are growing up around it. It's withered and is struggling, but it's still connected with the vine. As long as it's connected with the vine, there is hope. So what does the gardener do? He gently picks it up and untangles it from the weeds. He cleans it off and tenderly intertwines it with some of the other branches so that it can be held up and restored. The gardener's goal is to *airo* withering branches so that their connection can be strengthened and fruit can begin to grow.

When it's clear that your way hasn't worked for you and you find yourself covered in dirt and surrounded by weeds, there is a gardener with a graceful heart and gentle hands who longs to pick you up. As a once-withered branch myself, I'm immensely grateful for the kind of gardener God is. He saw me in the dirt, gently picked me up with graceful hands, cleaned me off, and placed me where I could grow and experience life once again.

I was speaking at an event where I had the opportunity to meet a man I'll call Adam. Adam shared with me that a number of years ago, he had spent some time in prison. He didn't say what he had been convicted of, and I didn't ask. When he went into prison, he was illiterate, unable to read or write. But another inmate, who was a Christian, offered to teach Adam to read by using the Bible. This inmate spent hours and hours teaching Adam to read. Eventually, Adam not only learned to read about Jesus, but he became a follower of Jesus. Adam said that when he was released, he tried to get connected with a church in the small town where he lived. But people in the church found out about his background, and a number of them felt uncomfortable with him being there. They didn't think he belonged with the "healthy branches."

One prominent family—longtime members of the church who to all appearances had produced all kinds of fruit—finally told the pastor he would need to ask Adam to go or they were going to leave. In their minds, it was time for Adam to officially be cut off. The pastor explained to this family that Jesus had come for people like Adam. The family ended up leaving, and others threatened to follow. Adam started thinking that maybe he had made too much of a mess of his life and that he ought to disconnect from God and the church.

One Sunday night after the sermon, the pastor asked Adam to come up front. Adam immediately knew what was going to happen. He was sure the pastor had found out about his crimes and was going to tell everyone—and then cut him off. He made his way to the front with his head down. He was so ashamed over what was about to happen. Some of the church members present at the service wanted Adam to leave, but they wished the pastor would just remove him quietly. It'd be less awkward that way.

When Adam reached the front, the pastor said he needed to talk to the church about a decision he had made. He explained that since being released, Adam had not been able to find work. The pastor said, "I brought Adam up here because I wanted to offer him a job. Adam, I'd like to hire you to help take care of the church facilities." And then the pastor put his hand in his pocket and pulled out an extra set of church keys and told Adam the keys were for him so he could open and close the church on Sundays.

As Adam is telling me his story, tears are running down his cheeks. He told me he had never had a key to anything his entire life. He felt loved and accepted. He felt picked up and connected. By the way, I should mention where I met Adam. I wasn't speaking at a prison; I was speaking at a pastors conference. Adam had been handed the keys to the church six years earlier, and he's now a pastor at that church.

I don't know what you would do with you or what others would do with you, but I know what God wants to do with you. No matter how spiritually dry or dead you might feel, no matter how unproductive your life has been, no matter how long you've been lying in the dirt and caught up in the weeds, God wants to gently pick you up and clean you off.

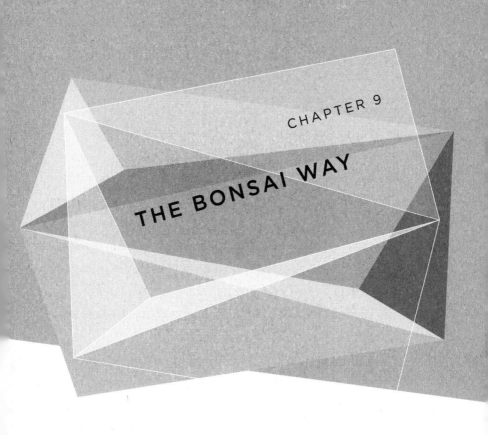

CHAPTER 9

THE BONSAI WAY

The 1980s were a wonderful time to be alive . . . cinematographically speaking. Ignore the eruption of Mount St. Helens and the Cold War and big hair with bigger bangs. Just think about the classic movies. The '80s gave us not only the *Goonies* but also the *Gremlins*. What about *The Princess Bride*? *E.T.*? The original *Indiana Jones* trilogy? Did you ever watch *The NeverEnding Story*?[1] One of my favorites from this era was the original *Karate Kid*, with Ralph Macchio as Daniel LaRusso and not-Jackie Chan[2] as Mr. Miyagi.

There's a scene in *The Karate Kid* where Daniel, the

---

1. If you try to watch it now, you realize why it's called *The NeverEnding Story*.
2. Pat Morita would think that was funny.

SECTION 2: THE WAY OF CONNECTION

teenage protagonist, walks into a room to find Mr. Miyagi, his octogenarian karate trainer. This time, he's not killing flies with chopsticks, which, by the way, isn't easy. Instead, Daniel finds Mr. Miyagi pruning a bonsai tree. Daniel watches as Mr. Miyagi cuts and snips away at the little plant. It's already small, but he keeps on pruning it anyway. Daniel isn't sure what Mr. Miyagi is trying to accomplish. He doesn't understand why this particular plant is getting cut. Mr. Miyagi attempts to include Daniel in the pruning process, but Daniel is afraid he'll make a mistake and kill the plant. To relieve his fear, Mr. Miyagi asks Daniel to close his eyes, eliminate distractions, and "think only tree."

Daniel envisions a beautiful bonsai tree in his mind, opens his eyes, and then trims and prunes the actual tree into alignment with the vision. Daniel learns that tending to a bonsai tree is an art that takes incredible time and skill. Depending on the artist, a bonsai tree can be worth a lot of money. One particular bonsai tree sold for $1.3 million. But it's different from a typical piece of art—it has to be continually nurtured, pruned, and cultivated. In the movie, Daniel discovers that he has to trust the mental picture of the tree's potential or he'll be too afraid to trim, cut, or prune any part.

In John 15, God is described as a good gardener who is always pruning. When your way isn't working and you're connected with the vine, you have to trust the picture the pruner has in mind. When you're the one being cut, you

146

instinctively question every clip. But God is not arbitrarily cutting and snipping; he has a picture in mind. Being the branch means learning not to resist his pruning so that we can more fully experience the beautiful and fruitful life he envisions for us.

Sometimes the pruning God does is noticeable to us and obvious to others. Sometimes the pruning involves small snips that aren't noticed in the moment but over time begin to shape and form us. God is a gardener who is continually pruning and bringing us more into alignment with his heart and vision. He has a picture in his mind, and we can trust his picture, even in the pruning.

Pruning 101

> He cuts off every branch in me that bears no fruit, while every branch that does bear fruit he prunes so that it will be even more fruitful.
>
> —JOHN 15:2

We've already talked about the first part of this verse and that tricky word *airo*, which means "to cut off" or "to lift up." As a reminder, while it can mean that God "cuts off" branches that are dead and only appear to be connected with the vine, most vineyard owners would translate this as "lift up" or "pick up" because they know that to care for a branch, you have to pick it up. You have to lift it up off the ground so that it can be fruitful. That's God's response to the struggling branches that are connected with the vine.

But what about the branches that are connected with the vine and *are* bearing fruit? They look healthy and seem productive. Common sense might dictate that they should be left alone so they can continue to grow. Jesus says that God *prunes* those branches so they "will be even more fruitful."

Since 2003, Matthiasson Wines has been producing high-quality wines in the Napa region. In a post on their website, the Matthiassons explain how they prune their vineyards:

> Why do we prune? Because if the vine is not pruned it reverts very quickly to its wild nature, climbing every-where with its long sinewy trunk and tiny scraggly bunches of uneven grapes. Every year we need to assess the growth of the vines, and decide whether to prune them back harder, or to let them grow a bit bigger, or return them to the same size and shape they were the year before.[3]

This pruning is clearly not a "cutting off"; it's a "cutting back." It is pruning with a purpose. The language of "getting cut" is almost never used in a positive connotation. Your vacation was *cut* short by an illness. You were *cut* from

---

3. "Pruning the Vines," Matthiasson Wines, www.matthiasson.com/pruning-the -vines-our-favorite-time-of-year, accessed December 16, 2022.

the team. Your company issued widespread pay *cuts*. Your "friends" *cut* you out of their plans or lives altogether. Work is *cutting* into your time with family because you're dealing with the consequences of a coworker *cutting* corners. You had to *cut* back on social interaction because of an illness. And all the while, it feels like no one is *cutting* you any slack.

Pruning sounds negative and painful, and it can be. Most of us are comfortable with the little cuts—some minor pruning in parts of our lives where we don't really notice it. Like when you get a haircut and tell the barber, "I need a haircut, but I don't want anyone to notice." But apparently that type of pruning generally isn't the most effective way to care for a plant or bring fruitfulness. Dr. Leonard Perry, a botanist who served as an extension horticulture specialist at the University of Vermont before his retirement, asserts that the biggest mistake gardeners and growers make is not pruning enough. In his opinion, at least 70 percent of the previous growth should be removed. That's a big chunk! So when it feels like God is chopping a big chunk of what we love or were looking forward to—or what we've at least become comfortable with—it can be painful.

A man in our church recently shared his experience with the pain of pruning. He had worked for the same company for nearly three decades. He had stuck with them through the economic ups and downs and had planned to retire from there. One day, he went into the office and was summoned into a meeting room, where he was told there were some cutbacks and his position was going to be eliminated. He would need to clean out his desk and turn in his key card by the end of the day. He found a box and collected the things that belonged to him. Someone from Human Resources came by, checked what was in his box, and walked him out to his car. He drove home in a daze, trying to make sense of what had just happened. Financially he would be okay, but this wasn't the picture he had in mind of what his future would look like. He felt rejected, betrayed, and embarrassed.

I should tell you where he shared his story with me. I was visiting a camp for disabled kids, and he was one of the volunteers that week. He wasn't lamenting or even complaining about losing his job; he related the story with a tone of gratitude. He loved to make a difference in the lives of these kids, and he now had the time to do it. Something he cared about and had invested in had been cut from his life. It was painful at first, but then a different picture began to come into focus.

Painful but Not Punishment

Pruning feels painful, but it's not punishment. That's difficult to accept. We tend to think that anything painful that happens against our will is punishment. The dilemma, then, is that if we see pruning and refinement as punishment, we will resist it at all costs. Instead of receiving it, we will resent it and rebel against it.

The Old Testament man named Job had all kinds of

things cut out of his life—his business, his family, his wealth, his physical health. As the story unfolds, his friends become aware of his suffering and basically ask him, "Hey, Job, what did you do to make God mad at you?" His wife blames God for making their lives miserable and concludes that Job's response should be to "curse God and die!" (Job 2:9).

Yet what we see in John 15 and understand about the pruning process is that painful things are not always punishment. When cherished pieces of our lives are being removed or our plans are being cut away, it may not be because God is punishing us. It could simply be that he is pretty good at pruning. He's got a picture in his mind, and we can trust him in the pruning. The logical questions, then, become these: "If pruning isn't punishment, what is it? What's the point of the pruning; what is God's purpose in it?"

Practices of Pruning

A branch that is connected with the vine will produce various shoots and leaves, and it seems as though there are certain "shoots and leaves" in our lives that God cuts back and prunes. We can separate these into three categories.

Diseased and Dying Shoots

First, God prunes some of the diseased and dying shoots in our lives. Think along the lines of secret sins, toxic relationships, and hurtful habits—patterns that have begun to infect our lives and, in turn, the lives of those around us.

God knows that continuing to live in this way isn't going to work, and so he prunes what is dying and diseased. Like a surgeon removing a cancerous tumor from the body, God prunes malignant growth when it starts to show up in our lives.

He prunes us through the Holy Spirit who lives in us. In the next chapter of John, Jesus tells his followers, "When he, the Spirit of truth, comes, he will guide you into all the truth" (John 16:13). The Holy Spirit makes us aware that our way isn't working. He shows us the areas of our lives that aren't aligned with God's ways. His approach is often called the "conviction of the Spirit." God prunes us of some of our diseased and dying attitudes through the conviction of the Spirit.

Think of a time you have experienced this. It's the jolt from a spiritual defibrillator that awakens your comatose soul when you've settled into rhythms of sinfulness. You're suddenly struck by a moment of clarity and you realize that the way you're living your life isn't what's best for you and it grieves the heart of God.

He prunes some of our diseased and dying shoots or leaves by exposing them. He takes what resides in the dark and brings it into the light. The addiction is no longer a secret, the texts get discovered, an idol gets uncovered, or lies are found out. God prunes through loving exposure. It becomes obvious, not only to us, but also to those around us, that our way isn't working. It can be embarrassing, costly, and life-altering, but God is far more concerned about our eternal health than our temporary comfort.

One of the most common ways God prunes and refines us is through the counsel of others who love and know us well enough to see when things aren't healthy. Someone sits down with us and we can tell that they're almost as uncomfortable as we are. They clearly don't want to have this conversation, but their love for us won't allow them to stay silent.

I recently took part in an exercise where I asked ten people I lead with to each give me two or three areas where they saw a need for growth in my life. One out of the ten had no problem with this request and quickly rattled off a half dozen areas that needed attention. It was as if this person had been waiting and preparing for this moment . . . our entire married lives. Two of the ten gave me some honest answers that weren't too hard for me to hear because these two men regularly speak into my life. The remaining seven used it as a time to encourage me and indicated that nothing obvious came to mind. I knew that wasn't true; they were just trying to be kind. I told them, "I know you want to encourage me, and I appreciate it, but I believe I'm in a season of pruning and I'm asking you to help me by telling me where you see room for growth."

I discovered that all ten of them had something to share. Most of them wouldn't have shared anything unless I handed them the pruning shears and insisted. An unanticipated benefit of that exercise was that not only did it help me see areas where I needed growth, but it also deepened my connection with each of them. In fact, I would say it was the least lonely I have felt in a long time. I thought I would feel criticized, but I felt cared for. There is something especially connecting when we realize someone sees us for who we are and yet still loves us.

Maybe you won't ask ten people to tell you what areas you need to work on, but my guess is you will have opportunities to choose how you will respond to counsel that is difficult to hear. Will you be easily offended and sensitive? Most of us are quick to become defensive. "Oh, is *that* what we're doing? We're calling each other out on our annoying habits, pointing out each other's mistakes? I didn't know. But two can play this game." And we pull out our pruning shears.

We go on the counterattack. When we respond like that, though, we resist the pruning that needs to take place and miss an opportunity to grow in Christlikeness. God desires to prune the dead and dying shoots and leaves from our lives, but it takes a certain level of humility and attentiveness to receive it.

Sucker Shoots

If we look closely at where a branch connects with a vine, it's not unusual to see sucker shoots growing around that area. The sucker shoots won't grow to bear fruit; rather, they will steal nutrients from the vine that should be going to fruit-bearing branches. The sucker shoots may seem harmless and not appear destructive, but they are distracting and steal the energy needed for the branch to bear fruit.

I asked my friends for examples of how God had pruned sucker shoots from their lives. A buddy told me his obsession with the news had become an unhealthy distraction. He would check it first thing in the morning and just before going to bed at night, as well as get constant notifications on his phone giving the latest headlines. He would even read the comments section in the news stories. That's when you know you have a problem.

A couple in our group said that a sucker shoot for their family had become youth sports. The daily practices and weekend tournaments were leaving them too busy, too worn-out to have the energy to connect with God and each other.

A friend of mine told me that when he got the "screen time" feature on his phone, it became clear that he needed to do some pruning. He realized how much time he was spending streaming on Netflix, surfing on Instagram, and watching YouTube shorts. He realized that each of these apps was like a sucker shoot that needed to be pruned.

Sucker shoots require constant pruning and maintenance. The moment you prune one, it will start to grow back or a new one will pop up in its place. It's a never-ending battle that needs our involvement.

Healthy Branches

Strangely enough, God prunes not only the diseased and dying branches but also the healthy fruit-bearing branches.

Why? Any gardener could answer that question. Sometimes a gardener must cut away something good to make room for better and more abundant fruit. This is the pruning that Jesus is talking about to his disciples when he says that every branch in him that bears fruit will be pruned (see John 15:2). Even though we may be spiritually healthy and bearing fruit, even though our way may seem to be working, God still prunes us because the picture he has in mind is a picture of Jesus, and none of us are there yet.

In the moment, pruning the healthy and fruitful branches feels counterintuitive. Why would someone cut away existing fruit in hopes of fruit that doesn't currently exist? That feels not just counterintuitive but counterproductive as well. However, Jesus explains that every branch that bears fruit will be pruned "so that it will be even more fruitful."

Jesus doesn't prune or refine us so that we'll be happy. It's not like God cut away your relationship with that guy you said had a "good personality" because he's got a far more attractive man with the same sense of humor waiting around the corner for you. While this scenario isn't outside the realm of possibility, this is not God's primary purpose in pruning.

He doesn't prune us so that we can become more successful by worldly standards. *God, is that why you've taken this job from me? Is it because you see a better-paying job on the horizon?* Again, it's possible, but don't presume that God is working off the current cultural definition of fruitfulness. No, he has a picture in his mind as he prunes, and the fruit that is pictured is "love, joy, peace, patience, kindness, goodness, faithfulness, gentleness, and self-control" (Galatians 5:22–23 NLT).

He prunes us for our ultimate good. Ultimately, what's truly good for us is not always what appears or feels "good" in this world. What's truly good for us is living in intimate relationship with God, the source of all goodness. A few verses later in John 15, Jesus also shows us that God prunes us for his glory: "This is to my Father's glory, that you bear much fruit, showing yourselves to be my disciples" (v. 8). God prunes us for our ultimate good and his ultimate glory.

Pruning has a purpose, and pruning is preparing us for something productive. When does that happen? Glad you asked. Well, that comes . . . later. It would be nice if the timeline were more specific and predictable. But waiting often gives us the best opportunity to practice abiding.

Wait until Later

A few years ago, I made an appointment with a professional landscaper to come to my house to plant a tree. And while he was there, he pruned our rose bushes out of the kindness of his heart . . . or out of pity because he could tell how badly they needed to be pruned. I had never hired a professional landscaper to prune our rosebushes. We had done some pruning on our bushes before, but we'd typically do it in the winter when no roses were in bloom. My reasoning was that if there were beautiful roses growing, what's the sense in cutting them off? The point of having a rosebush is so you can have roses, is it not? So why would you cut off the roses? I was shocked at how many roses the landscaper pruned and how short he cut back the bushes.

I was skeptical that this guy knew what he was doing, and I expressed some of my frustration to him about it. "Dude, you cut off all the roses!"

He replied, "Yeah, it's part of the pruning process." He explained it to me, recognizing how little I knew. He sensed I was a little annoyed, so he said, "Look, I know it doesn't seem to make sense now, but wait until later. Trust me, I know what I'm doing." Then he got out his phone and showed me some pictures of his landscaping work. He has a picture in mind each time he does his pruning—a picture of flourishing rosebushes with more roses every year.

"It doesn't make sense now, but wait until later." Maybe that's the message of the Gardener to you these days. You may not be able to understand exactly what God is forming in you or bringing about through you, "but wait until later." Right now, it just feels like the Lord is doing a lot of cutting and pruning, but there's a picture we can't completely see yet. What's been taken from you may feel counterintuitive and counterproductive, "but wait until later."

Snips or the Chainsaw

Here's the challenge: If it's true that pruning isn't punishment or pointless but rather is completely purposeful . . . ask for it. Ask for the pruning. If Jesus' portrayal of pruning is accurate, we shouldn't merely accept it or tolerate it; we should ask for it. Over the years, I've discovered the hard way that the pruning we ask for isn't nearly as painful as the pruning we don't ask for.

I would rather invite the consistent snips of God's sovereign scissors than wait until a chainsaw is required to restore me to health. Pruning should be a continual, consistent process. Part of what makes being engaged in a local body of believers so important is that it's the environment in which we can best invite God's pruning into our lives. You may be prone to avoiding church attendance or Bible reading because these disciplines always challenge your thoughts and desires . . . but that's kind of the point. To consistently be challenged, encouraged, affirmed, and convicted is better than living a carefree life until God, out of love, has to pull out the STIHL MS 271 Farm Boss chainsaw. Ask for the pruning. The one who holds the scissors is trustworthy. He's got a picture in his mind. We can trust him in the pruning.

To get super practical with this, if you're willing to accept Jesus' teaching on pruning and trust God's picture for your life, think about praying these words:

O Lord,

Are there some dead and diseased branches in my life that need to go? Is there an addiction for which I need to get some help? Is there a toxic relationship that isn't honoring you? Is there something secretive that you need to pull into the light? God, are there some thought patterns that I've allowed to go unchecked? Are there some things that I've given my eyes and attention to that have stunted the growth you want to see in me?

God, is there some bitterness that is poisoning the branch, keeping me from being fully connected with you and poisoning the fruit you want to grow in my life? Is there someone I need to forgive, someone I need to give grace to? Is there an offense I need to overlook? Is there some anger that needs to be released? God, do I need to prune some voices in my life? Would you reveal to me the voices I need to stop listening to?

God, are there some fears and insecurities that are holding me back from bearing the fruit that you want to see grow in me, that I need to surrender to you once and for all? Are there some good things on my schedule that need to be pruned so I can be available for the better things that you're wanting to produce in and through me? If so, God, would you pry them from my white-knuckled grip so that I can be the person you've made me to be? What do you need to cut back in my life because it's holding me back from what you've called me to do?

God, I believe you are the good Gardener. Would you prune some of what's good because you have a better picture in mind for me? May I not refuse or resist the pruning, but instead have the faith to invite it and receive it, trusting that your pruning has a purpose and is getting me closer to the picture you have in mind.

It's in Jesus' name I pray.

Amen.

CHAPTER 10

TANGLED UP

S ome things we cannot do alone. In fact, there are some things we aren't meant to do alone. Take the game Marco Polo, for example. The tagger, who has their eyes closed, shouts "Marco!" and all the other players shout "Polo!" Then the tagger tries to capture another player by using just their sense of hearing. You can't really play that game by yourself.[1] You'd probably be waiting for a really long time for someone else to join the game and say, "Polo!"

What about having a conversation? Can you have a

---

1. Although why don't you try. Wherever you are right now, shout "Marco" and see what happens. You might be surprised.

conversation by yourself? You can, but it may concern your friends. How about a proper handshake? Set this book down for a second and try to shake your own hand without looking like a crazy person.[2] It's impossible.

Some things just don't work the way they should when you try to do them alone—riding a seesaw, applying sunscreen to the middle of your back, going to Chuck E. Cheese as a grown adult, singing a duet, playing frisbee, and, I would add, staying connected with the Vine.

No Solo Branches

As we read Jesus' Farewell Discourse and consider his words, we find that he is speaking to his disciples with the assumption that they will do this together. When our way isn't working, we may tend to want to withdraw and isolate, but Jesus is calling us to stay connected with the vine by staying connected with the other branches.

Notice this small but important detail when Jesus introduces the metaphor of the vine in John 15:5: "I am the vine; you are the branches." Did you catch it? Jesus doesn't say, "I am the vine; you are the branch." He says, "You are the *branches*." It's plural. In our effort to personalize Scripture, we sometimes read it through an individualistic lens, but this isn't Jesus sitting at a "table for two" having a one-on-one conversation; this is Jesus in the locker room

---

2. If you shouted "Marco" while shaking your own hand, we would get along great.

talking to the entire team. His followers are called to follow him *together*.

If you go to a natural vineyard that has a simple trellis system and walk up and down the rows of vines and branches, you will find that the branches are tangled together. The branches are not tied in knots, but they weave around one another. This network of tangled branches gives strength and support to each individual branch. As the newer, younger branches begin to grow, they weave themselves around the stronger, more mature branches so they can be held up and begin to bear fruit. A branch that is solo, even one that is connected with the vine, needs to be tangled with other branches or it will soon be down in the dirt.

We tend to underestimate this aspect of being the branch. The individualized nature of our Western culture can easily infiltrate our approach to faith. A Dutch social psychologist named Geert Hofstede conducted a study that measured, among other things, the degree to which individuals of a given country were integrated into groups and communities. He translated his findings into a scale that gives a score to each nation studied based on how individualistic their citizens tended to be.[3]

You want to guess where the United States ranks? With a score of 91 on the Hofstede Scale of Individualism, the United States ranks number one as the world's most individualistic

---

3. See "The Pros and Cons of America's (Extreme) Individualism," *Freakonomics Radio*, July 21, 2021, https://freakonomics.com/podcast/the-pros-and-cons-of -americas-extreme-individualism-ep-470-2.

nation. What's fascinating, though, is to look at how abnormal that level of individualism is across the world. Of the sixty-five other nations studied, fifty-five of them scored lower than 70. The average score was right around 39.[4]

If you live in the United States, chances are you don't understand what the problem is. In fact, we tend to wear our individualism as a badge of honor. We're quite sure we don't need help, and if we're really uncertain about what to do, we can always ask our friends Siri, Google, or Alexa. We've never had a more individualistic approach. And we've never been more lonely.

Counterfeit Connections

What contributes to the loneliness is not just our individualism but also that the connections we do have with people aren't very deep. Culturally, the way we use the word *connection* is often in the context of our phones, and by that definition, we've never been more connected. I read an article in the *New York Times* called "The Rise of the Toilet Texter" revealing that 75 percent of smartphone users are on their phones while in the bathroom. For those eighteen to twenty-eight, the number was 91 percent, though they're not typically making phone calls. What's really crazy is that nearly 25 percent of Americans said they wouldn't go to

---

4. See "Geert Hofstede Cultural Dimensions: Individualism," Clearly Cultural, https://clearlycultural.com/geert-hofstede-cultural-dimensions/individualism, accessed December 16, 2022.

the bathroom without their phones.[5] Again, 25 percent of
Americans say, *I'm not going in there alone. That's crazy.* All of
our texting and social media relationships have revealed the
deep longing and need we have for something more.

In 2008, Hal Niedzviecki wrote a *New York Times* maga-
zine article in which he reflected on the current state of his
online friends.[6] He had seven hundred friends on Facebook
alone. Hal wrote that he was "absurdly proud of how many
cyberpals, connections, acquaintances and even strangers I'd
managed to sign up." But he went on to admit that because
of a two-year-old at home, his "workaholic irritability," and
his love for alone time, he had fewer in-the-flesh friends to
hang out with than he used to.

To celebrate his virtual friends, Hal decided to throw a
Facebook party to spend some in-person time with them.
He sent an invitation to all seven hundred of his friends. He
asked them to meet up a local bar. His friends could respond
in one of three options: "Attending," "Maybe Attending,"
and "Not Attending." Fifteen said they would be there,
and sixty said they might be there. He guessed somewhere
around twenty would show up.

He writes about what happened next: "On the evening in
question, I took a shower. I shaved. I splashed on my tingly man
perfume. I put on new pants and a favorite shirt. Brimming

5. Cited in Quentin Hardy, "The Rise of the Toilet Texter," *New York Times,* January
30, 2012, https://archive.nytimes.com/bits.blogs.nytimes.com/2012/01/30/the
-rise-of-the-toilet-texter.
6. Hal Niedzviecki, "Facebook in a Crowd," *New York Times,* October 7, 2008,
www.nytimes.com/2008/11/07/opinion/07iht-edniedzviecki.1.17624519.html.

with optimism, I headed over to the neighborhood watering hole and waited. And waited. And waited. Eventually, one person showed up." And who was the one person who came? Hal didn't know her. Turns out she was a friend of a friend. They chatted for a few minutes before she left. Hal waited until midnight, but no one else showed up. So he ordered a beer and sat by himself. He concludes his article with these words: "Seven hundred friends, and I was drinking alone."

Sherry Turkle, a professor at MIT and author of *Alone Together*, has spent the last fifteen years studying how our "plugged-in lives" have changed who we are. She claims that all of our technological devices have produced a world in which we're always communicating but seldom having real conversations. She describes social media as taking little "sips" and thinking we are getting plenty to drink, while in reality we are dehydrated. She explains that social media offers the illusion of companionship without the demands of a relationship.[7] She reminds us that social media offers the illusion of connection without the demands of commitment, and connection without commitment leaves us feeling lonelier than ever.

According to the *American Journal of Preventive Medicine*, people who reported spending the most time on social media—more than two hours a day—had twice the odds of feelings of isolation compared to those who spent a half hour or less. People who visited social media platforms most frequently—fifty-eight visits per week or more—had more than three times

---

7. See Sherry Turkle, *Alone Together: Why We Expect More from Technology and Less from Each Other* (New York: Basic Books, 2012), 1.

the odds of feelings of isolation and loneliness compared to those who visited fewer than nine times per week.[8]

How do we know if a connection is significant or superficial? Here are some signs of a superficial connection.

You communicate information but not feelings. The person is not someone you feel safe to be honest and vulnerable with. You exchange information about your job, your kids, your fantasy football team, or your latest redecorating project, but you do not share your emotions. You might trade information about other people's messes, but you don't talk about your own mess. You don't express the frustration you're experiencing in your marriage, the fears you have around finances, the anger you feel toward your kids, the temptation you're struggling with, or the anxiety you feel over a big decision.

You don't know details about the person's life. My wife has helped me recognize this truth. I'll spend the afternoon with a friend and come home and my wife will ask about his wife and I'll say, "I'm not really sure how she's doing. We didn't really talk about it?" My wife doesn't understand: "You spent the entire afternoon together and you never asked about his wife? What *did* you talk about?" *I don't know. Nothing, I guess.* A test of connection is in the details.

You only connect if one of you needs something. If your phone rings and you see that person's name, you know they're not just calling to check in and see how you're doing. They

8. Cited in Katherine Hobson, "Feeling Lonely? Too Much Time on Social Media May Be Why," NPR, March 6, 2017, www.npr.org/sections/health-shots/2017/03/06/518362255/feeling-lonely-too-much-time-on-social-media-may-be-why.

have a question about something or are calling for information. It's just a transactional relationship.

You've never had to overcome a personal conflict. Until a relationship goes through some conflict, the connection won't be strengthened. I've heard this referred to as going through the "tunnel of chaos" with someone. In the tunnel of chaos, you speak truth to one another, even the hard stuff. You don't know what's going to happen in the tunnel of chaos. You may encounter rejection, hurt feelings, or arguments, but it's worth the risk because on the other side is a deeper and more authentic connection.

You wouldn't call the person if you needed help. If you need a ride to the airport, have gotten sick and need a hand taking care of a few things, or need accountability to take on a new habit, you wouldn't ask this person for help. I've read that the way you find out how many of your virtual friends are real friends is to post that you're moving and need help and see who shows up—in other words, when you're facing something difficult. When life isn't working the way you had hoped it would, who shows up?

Tangled Together

If we're going to experience life the way Jesus wants us to experience it on this side of heaven, living in community isn't optional. In his teaching about the vine and the branches, Jesus gives a clear command to his disciples in John 15:12: "My command is this: Love each other as I have loved you."

170

Jesus calls us to live in radically love-filled relationships with one another because he knows that our souls need it, even as we fully recognize that our sinfulness will make it difficult. Living an individual, isolated life may be what's easiest in a particular moment or season, but it's dangerous and is difficult to sustain over a lifetime. There is an old African proverb that goes like this: "If you want to go fast, go alone; if you want to go far, go together."

From the beginning, God made it clear that we were made for connection with others. In Genesis, we read of the creation of the world. In Genesis 1:26, God said, "Let us make mankind in our image." So who's he talking to?

The point is that God is not alone. He's talking to Jesus and the Holy Spirit: "Let us make mankind in *our* image." Part of being made in God's image is being made for community. We read again and again in the creation account that God declares, "It is good"—until we get to Genesis 2, when God creates the man, and he looks at him and says, "It is not good for the man to be alone" (v. 18). As the architect and designer of mankind, God has created us for connection. He's created us for meaningful and significant relationships. He looks at a life that is lived with complete independence and self-reliance and says, "*That* is not good."

Allelon

The New Testament uses a particular word frequently that helps us understand the good that God has in mind. It reveals how God wants us to be connected as branches who stay connected with the vine. Living life as tangled branches can sometimes be messy, but it's all part of living a meaningful life. In John 15, Jesus tells his followers to be the branches and love one another. As the rest of the New Testament unfolds, the Greek word *allelon* (*al-lay-lone*) shows us what his command looks like in practice—translated into English as "each other" or "one another."

Tracing *allelon* throughout the New Testament and meditating on a few of its specific uses gives us insight into our messy and meaningful connections. *Allelon* is used some one hundred times in the New Testament, and it's often preceded by a practical relationship principle of some sort: "*serve* one another," "*forgive* each other," "*submit* to one another," "*pray* for each other," "*encourage* one another," "*comfort* one another." Studying all of those imperatives is a book of its own. But for the purpose of our connection conversation, I want to draw your attention to a couple of the ways the word *allelon* helps us be the branches.

Accept One Another

Accept one another, then, just as Christ accepted you, in order to bring praise to God.

—ROMANS 15:7

This verse is a helpful starting point as we seek to live life on the vine with other branches because we can't create community without accepting our differences. Our increasingly tribal approach to community creates a pressure to reject people from other tribes.

When I became the senior pastor at our church, I wanted to address some of the disunity that I believed was hurting the connections and community of our staff. The source of disunity wasn't political disagreements, eschatological interpretations, or ecclesiology matters. It was much more serious than that. We were experiencing a bitter division between the two major types of coffee drinkers.

There is a certain segment of us who really like cheap coffee. I'm a gas station coffee guy. I just need some caffeine. If I don't feel like splurging at a coffee shop, I'm content with using the Keurig with the Great Value version of a K-Cup. So there's that group of us. We called that group "the Followers."

But then there's the other group, the other side. Let's just call them the coffee snobs or coffee elitists, or simply "the Fans." They're skeptical of getting their coffee from any institution that is a chain with multiple locations. So they only frequent the little hole-in-the-wall café that imports their beans from the newly discovered, organically grown rainforest on one of Jupiter's moons. They're the kind of people who grind their own beans and know how to do the complicated pour over method. They have a half dozen apparatuses and devices that are involved in the process, but none of them are a coffee maker! My guess is these are the same practitioners of the dark arts who mow the checkered pattern in their lawns.

As one of the elders at church, I wanted to bridge the chasm between the two different coffee camps and bring unity to our community. It was time to get these branches tangled together. So I decided I was going to compromise and attempt to understand the perspective of the other side. I looked up the address of one of the coffee shops that everyone raved about and made the pilgrimage to this temple where these people go to worship.

I walked into the little shop, and immediately I felt like I didn't belong. Apparently, I wasn't wearing the proper head gear for this coffee cult—a beanie and AirPods. When the barista[9] asked for my order, I tried to just parrot exactly what my friend had told me to order: "I'll have an expresso."

"Do you mean *espresso?*" the guy behind the counter questioned.

I was like, "Aren't we . . . Aren't we saying the same thing?"

He said, "You said *expresso.* I think you meant *espresso.*"

I started to panic. I was a little intimidated, so I just switched my order to a large coffee. I felt confident in the simplicity of that order.

But then he surprised me with another question: "Well, what origin do you want?"

I didn't have any idea what he was talking about. I wanted to say, "7-Eleven" or "Love's Travel Stop," but I was sure those weren't the right answers. I just ended up asking,

---

9. He was a dude, so is it *baristo?*

"What do you recommend?" with the slightest hint of a French accent.

He recommended the Peruvian Single Origin Coffee.

Clearly, I didn't know what that was, which led the barista to try to convince me further: "You can taste the soil."

Of course I want to taste the dirt from Peru in my coffee. Because that's a good thing. Weary from the whole interaction, I went ahead and accepted his suggestion, transferred some money from savings over to my debit card, and ordered the coffee. I took a sip. It was as bitter and dark as the coffee shop. I asked the barista where I could find the cream and sugar, which I've since learned is the equivalent of going to a PETA convention and asking if anyone knows of a steak place that serves a good veal.[10] It's safe to say the division between the coffee simpletons and the coffee snobs remains.

You get the picture, right? It's a trivial example, but that sort of "us versus them" mentality is very real in our world. So real that I had to use a trivial example so I wouldn't divert all you readers from the point of this chapter by dividing you into tribes. There are different sides to almost every subject. We have different perspectives, approaches, dreams, desires, candidates, backgrounds, temptations, and on and on. It can feel like, no matter what side you're on, you're required to be opposed to the other side, whatever and whoever it may be. Being the branches changes all that. It means we accept one another, even if we don't fully agree with one another's

---

10. "Vincenzo's," if you're ever in Louisville, Kentucky.

opinions. We can accept a person without thinking that our acceptance of the person is an agreement with or an endorsement of everything they believe.

Lack of acceptance was a major issue in the early church as new believers learned to be tangled together. One example can be found in the book of Romans. Division surfaced in the church over the varying ethnic and religious backgrounds of the believers. Some of the Roman Christians came from a Jewish background and had always worshiped the one true God, endeavored to obey his commands, and followed a specific set of religious traditions, but now they recognized Jesus as the fulfillment of their Jewish faith. So they submitted to his teachings as their Messiah, their long-awaited King.

Other believers in the church in Rome came from a Gentile background. They grew up in a city where they worshiped a pantheon of gods, along with whomever the emperor happened to be at the time. They engaged in all sorts of evil religious practices out of superstitious devotion to false deities. Of course, they didn't think of themselves as superstitious, just a little *stitious*.[11] But now these Gentiles had heard the good news about Jesus and they chose to abandon their gods for the one true God. So the Jews are holding on to some of their traditions and the Gentiles are holding on to some of their superstitions. You see how things can get messy. Both sides naturally gravitated toward excluding the other from the church.

---

11. Michael Scott, regional manager at Dunder Mifflin (Scranton Branch).

So Paul writes this letter to the church in Rome and essentially lays out the basic message of the gospel: it doesn't matter who you are; you are sinful and unworthy of God's mercy. But God is more merciful than we are sinful, and out of his love for us, he has made salvation possible to all people through Jesus. We are all connected with the same vine, and that connection means we accept one another.

The goal is to live life in the meaningfully messy community that God has called us to, but community is not possible where acceptance is not present. If we're not able to accept followers of Jesus who look, talk, think, worship, vote, dress, and express themselves differently, we will never be able to experience a life on the vine that is intertwined with other branches. Then we can too easily settle for coexistence, which is a cheap substitute for meaningful community.

It's sometimes hard to accept others not because we disagree with them on certain issues but because, well, sometimes they *are* the issue. They are just ~~different~~ weird. I think a lot of solo branches are trying to stay connected with the vine on their own because they think the other branches are weird. Just like in most families, there will be certain people who are somewhat strange or a little high-maintenance.

Can I acknowledge something I think most of us are well aware of? There are some weird people who go to church. Certainly not the majority, but let's say in a church of a thousand, maybe 5 percent of people are weird. That's fifty weird people. That can feel like a lot of weirdness. Some of you are reading this and thinking, *I haven't noticed weird people around my church*. Ummm, I'm not sure how to say this . . . that probably means . . . *you* are the weird one. I've decided that most of these people would have been weird, even if they hadn't become Christians. I used to try to help weird people be less weird, but at some point, I accepted their weirdness. Because that's what a family does.

Bear One Another's Burdens

Galatians 6:2 (ESV) reads, "Bear one another's burdens, and so fulfill the law of Christ." A few years ago, a pastor friend of mine lost a child after a long battle with cancer. Recently, I was at a pastors conference with him. We were sitting at a table as people were registering. Another pastor walked in the room and began walking toward us. I had never met this pastor, but I knew who he was.

I said to my buddy, "I think he's coming over here. Do you know him?"

He shook his head no.

As the pastor approached, I could see some emotion in his face. In that moment, my friend who was sitting with me seemed to understand what was happening. He stood up, and the two of them embraced while the pastor we didn't know cried. It was a long hug.

After a few minutes, he introduced himself and explained that his daughter had recently been diagnosed with cancer. After he left, I asked my friend, "How did you know what that was about? Does that happen very often?"

He explained that after losing a child to cancer, they

discovered a unique and deep bond with others who experience similar devastation.

We discover a strength and a fruitfulness when we recognize that we aren't strong enough on our own. We need help. We need each other.

When a large package delivered to your house exceeds a certain weight limit, you'll usually see an image on the outside of the box. The picture shows two people picking up and carrying the box, which cues you that it's too heavy for one person to carry alone. So here's the question: Do you see the image as a *warning*: "Don't try to carry this on your own." Or do you see it as a *challenge*: "It takes two normal people to carry this box. Are you just a normal person?"

God has taught me and is continuing to teach me that spiritual maturity and courage mean doing life with others—being willing to share our burdens. It's something I've had to learn the hard way. When my way isn't working and I'm dealing with something that feels big and heavy, I have a hard time humbling myself and asking for help.

As I was writing this chapter, I began to reflect on how much God has taught me about my need for others. So I decided to take a few minutes to write notes of gratitude to some of the people in my life who helped bear my burdens in recent years. At the end of each note, I signed it with this Scripture reference—Galatians 5:2. I didn't write out the verse; I just wrote down the reference.

Well, I thought Galatians 5:2 said, "Bear one another's burdens, and so fulfill the law of Christ" (ESV). But about a week after sending those messages, I realized I had the reference wrong. The correct reference for that verse is Galatians 6:2, not Galatians 5:2. Galatians 5:2 reads, "Mark my words! I, Paul, tell you that if you let yourselves be circumcised, Christ will be of no value to you at all." So yeah, a little different from what I intended. I don't think any of them actually looked up the verse because no one said anything to me about it.

It's Galatians 6:2 that reminds us that we need one another and that God has made us for one another. When your way isn't working, it feels like some extra weight has been added to the load you have to carry through life. Your burden gets heavier—too heavy for you to carry alone.

In the middle of the COVID-19 pandemic, there were times when it seemed that every decision seemed to come with nothing but bad options. No matter what decision was made, no matter what you said or didn't say, people would get upset. I came home from work one day a little discouraged, and my wife said, "You should call and talk to one of your senior pastor friends who are dealing with the same stuff." But when she said it, it wasn't really a suggestion.

I sent a text to my childhood friend Jon Weece, who is the senior pastor of a similar church about an hour away. My text said, "Hey, man, it was a tough day today. It feels like it's one thing after another. Do you have a few minutes to talk?" I realize that most of you would say that sending a text like that isn't a big deal, but it was for me. Remember, I hate being perceived as weak and whiny, so reaching out for help was humbling.

An hour or so later, my phone rang. I looked down at the screen and saw that it was Jon. I picked it up and said "Hello . . ." On the other end of the phone, I hear a knowing laugh. I start laughing, and the two of us just laughed into the phone for a few minutes without really saying anything. We just understood what the other person was going through. We prayed and I hung up the phone. When I got off the phone, my wife asked me if our chat was helpful. I said, "Yeah, it was really helpful." She said, "What did you talk about?" I said, "Nothing."

I was reluctant to call Jon because I knew there was nothing he could say to change my situation. My way wasn't working, and neither was his, but we reminded each other that we weren't alone and that our hope is in Jesus.

The Greek word (*baros*) for "burdens" in Galatians 6:2 can be translated as "excessive weight." It's humbling to ask someone to help you bear your burdens, and it's hard to help bear the burdens of others, but if we aren't living this way, we're not fulfilling the way of Christ.

We were made for connection—not just for connection with Jesus but also with one another. Eugene Peterson put it this way: "I am not myself by myself."[12] Life doesn't work the way God intended it to work unless and until we are living in connection with others.

---

12. Eugene H. Peterson, *Christ Plays in Ten Thousand Places: A Conversation in Spiritual Theology* (Grand Rapids: Eerdmans, 2005), 226.

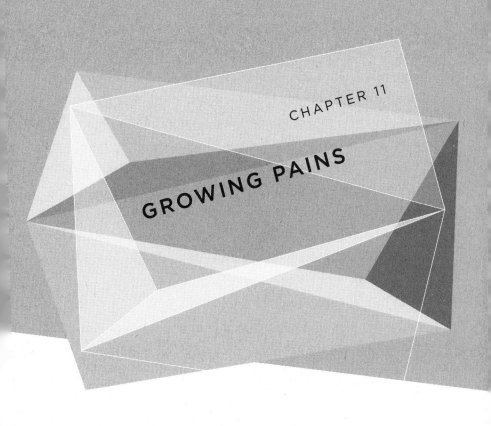

CHAPTER 11

GROWING PAINS

The wave of temptation may even wash you higher up upon the Rock of ages, so that you cling to it with a firmer grip than you have ever done before, and so again where sin abounds, grace will much more abound.

—Charles Spurgeon

Rock of ages" is a name for God used in the Old Testament.[1] Isaiah 26:4 reads, "Trust in the Lord (commit yourself to Him, lean on Him, hope confidently in Him) forever; for the Lord God is an

---

1. Also a 2012 musical starring Tom Cruise featuring a lot of lip-synching. But as I've said many times, Tom Cruise is no Milli Vanilli.

everlasting Rock [the *Rock of Ages*]" (AMPC). This verse reinforces the idea that Yahweh, our God, is a strong, immovable source of strength and security. Spurgeon uses the metaphor of a wave to help us understand the suffering and hardships we experience in this life. We sometimes talk about the struggles of life as if they're solely something to survive. Instead, God's Word teaches us to welcome the wave, to embrace the struggle, because God can use painful experiences to connect us with him in powerful ways. He can take up our struggle and help us find a new way that leads to life. According to 2 Corinthians 7:10 (TLB), "God sometimes uses sorrow in our lives to help us turn away from sin and seek eternal life."

Charles Spurgeon, the source of this thought-provoking image, was a preacher in the 1850s. He is said to have preached an average of thirteen times per week throughout the course of his ministry. There have been some 56 million publications of his sermons in nearly forty different languages.[2] He enjoyed incredible influence, but he also endured incredible suffering. He struggled with depression most of his life. Perhaps you know how debilitating depression can be, especially when it doesn't go away after a month or a year.

Like Spurgeon, maybe you've come to know depression as a constant companion. Spurgeon's wife was bedridden for about twenty-five years of their marriage. He spoke strongly

---

2. Cited in Michael Reeves, "Suffering Taught Him to Look to Christ: Charles Spurgeon 1834–1892," Desiring God, October 19, 2018, www.desiringgod.org /articles/suffering-taught-him-to-look-to-christ.

against American slavery and was persecuted as a result. Like the disciples in the first century, he faced intense opposition because of the boldness with which he preached the truth and applied it to the lives of the people around him.

Spurgeon shared what it was like to experience that sort of suffering, those waves of hardship:

> I have been cast into "waters to swim in," which, but for God's upholding hand, would have proved waters to drown in. I have endured tribulation from many flails. Sharp bodily pain succeeded mental depression, and this was accompanied both by bereavement, and affliction in the person of one dear to me as life [speaking of Susannah, his wife]. The waters rolled in continually, wave upon wave. I do not mention this to exact sympathy, but simply to let the reader see that I am no dry-land sailor. I have traversed full many a time those oceans which are not Pacific: I know the roll of the billows, and the rush of the winds. Never were the promises of Jehovah so precious to me as at this hour. Some of them I never understood till now.[3]

Spurgeon was fifty-three when he wrote that. In essence, he is saying, "I have experienced the waves of this world, and I can tell you that the waves have cast me upon the Rock of Ages—and for that I am grateful. I have come to know

---

3. C. H. Spurgeon, *Faith's Checkbook* (Christian Classics Ethereal Library), https://ccel.org/ccel/spurgeon/checkbook/checkbook.i.html, accessed January 10, 2023.

the power and presence of God in a way I would not have otherwise."

Suffering in this life can be a vehicle that either drives us away from Jesus or drives us closer to him. Spurgeon's kind of growth only happens if we will kiss the wave. If you're like me, when you find that your way isn't working and you start to experience some of the pain and hardships that go along with it, your first instinct is to get out of the water. But what if there is a connection you can only experience and a fruit that can only be produced during troubled times?

Mature through the Manure

We have been studying verses from John 15, which is in the middle of the Farewell Discourse—Jesus' final words to his closest followers. He is preparing them for challenges and hardships that he knows they will experience in this world. When the wind and waves begin to overtake them, the one thing they must do is stay connected with Jesus.

The Farewell Discourse begins and ends with a promise, which sounds a lot more like a warning, about the waves that are going to come. In John 14:1, Jesus says, "Do not let your hearts be troubled."

Oh, okay. So that's it then? Don't let my heart be troubled. Perfect. Thanks for the help, Jesus.

It's not like I want to have a troubled heart. I don't want to fall asleep at night thinking through contingency plans. I don't want to wake up in the morning overwhelmed with everything that's happening in the world and in my life. So the question is this: *How?* How do I not have a troubled heart?

Most of us make it about circumstances, but it's really all about connection. We think that having a troubled heart can only happen in the kiddie pool or the lazy river. We would probably say to Jesus, *Okay, if you don't want my heart to be troubled, then change my circumstances, solve my problem, and promise me that everything is going to be okay.*

Did you see the story in the news about the wave pool that malfunctioned at a water park in China? Forty-four people were injured, many with broken bones, when a huge wave was unleashed on an unsuspecting crowd enjoying a relaxing afternoon in what was normally a fairly calm and always well-controlled tsunami pool. There are different reports as to what went wrong. The water park blamed it on equipment failure, but it was widely reported that a drunken employee set the wave-making dial to its highest setting to see what would happen.[4] Either way, what's clear is that the people in charge lost control of what was happening, and a lot of people ended up hurt.[5]

That story happened in 2019, and ironically that's a year before it felt like someone turned up the wave-making dial on our world. The waves seemed to get bigger and come more frequently, and no one seemed to know what was

---

4. Something I would have a very hard time not being tempted to do when completely sober.
5. See Daisy Hernandez, "Wave Pool Suffers Huge Malfunction, Injures 44 People," *Popular Mechanics*, August 1, 2019, www.popularmechanics.com/about/a28567877/wave-pool.

going on. Maybe you wondered if God had lost control of things or if the angel in charge of the wave dial didn't have proper training. It all seemed like it was too much.

What made the situation at the water park in China especially dangerous is that people weren't expecting it. They didn't see it coming, so they weren't prepared when it happened. People panicked. Some of them tried to get out of the way, while others tried to grab hold of anything or anyone they could find. Jesus doesn't want his followers to be caught off guard, so he states clearly that they will have trouble. That's how the Farewell Discourse starts in John 14 and that's how it ends in chapter 16: "In this world you will have trouble" (v. 33).

The word for *trouble* here connotes severity. Jesus could have used other words for what could be described as annoyances or frustrations. That's not this. This is a word reserved for deep pain. For intense struggle. For overwhelming discouragement. And Jesus begins and ends his talk by making sure his followers understand that trouble is coming. He knows that if trouble comes and they aren't expecting it, they will feel disillusioned. Too often disillusionment leads to disconnection.

A number of years ago, my wife and I went white-water rafting with a group in Northern California. I was expecting it to be a few days of relaxing on a raft, laughing with friends, and taking in some beautiful scenery. When we arrived at the river, we were assigned a guide, who lined us up along the shore. He told us he wanted to prepare us for what we were about to face. He got our attention by beginning with a few horror stories of people who had gone on the expedition but hadn't paid close attention to his talk. We were listening as he described the class III and class IV rapids we would encounter. He warned us to look out for each other and to know what to do if the person we're sitting next to is tossed overboard.

When we finally got into the raft and started floating down calm waters, we kept practicing what we were supposed to do when the rapids came. We practiced listening to and responding to the guide's commands: *paddle backward, paddle forward, left back, right back, lean in.* It's the "lean in" command that sticks in my mind. If we hit an obstacle, came up on a steep drop, or hit a big wave, he would yell to *lean in.* Everyone was to lean in to the middle and grab hold of the safety line and not let go. There was no question that the rapids would come, and the guide wanted us to be prepared.

That's what Jesus is doing for his followers. He is warning them that trouble is coming, so they shouldn't be surprised when it does. When the big waves come, and they will, hang on and don't let go. Whatever happens, stay connected.

Expect and Expectant

As followers of Jesus, we accept a strange reality. Becoming a follower of Jesus is the first and most important step toward experiencing a restored life, free from the effects of our broken world and our sinful flesh. The tension is that before we experience total restoration, we're called to wait faithfully in a flawed realm. A majority of the Christian life consists of learning to wait well. As we wait, the waves of life are not just probable; they're certain.

When I was younger and one of our relatives or family friends would experience a tragedy or trial of some sort, my dad would say to my siblings and me, "Hey, our time is coming." That's a surefire way to give a kid nightmares and panic attacks. It's not a very positive or encouraging message, but it's true. My dad wanted us to be prepared for that time when the waves would come, so he'd gently remind us, "Our time is coming." That's what Jesus is doing in John 16. He's taking the surprise out of it, saying in essence, "Now that you're following me, don't expect life to get easier immediately. There will be waves." But Jesus doesn't just want us to get through the waves; he wants us to grow. If we stay connected with him, there is fruit on the other side. Don't just expect the trouble; be expectant in the trouble.

In John 16, Jesus further explains why he's warning them of the trouble that is coming and pleading with them to stay connected with him. He says in verse 1, "All this I have told you so that you will not fall away." Essentially, Jesus says to his closest followers, "I'm telling you these things, not because I'm trying to discourage you, not because I'm trying to scare you, not because I'm trying to make you feel insecure and unconfident; I'm telling you these things because I don't want you to fall away."

Then in verse 2 he talks more specifically about the waves

that are coming: "They will put you out of the synagogue"—
the place where you most want to be admired, they're gonna
kick you out of. The group of friends you grew up with,
the people at work you really want to like you—they're not
gonna accept you anymore. Jesus is warning them about
what is to come, but don't forget that the context of this
warning is that *good things will come.* Remember that when
people treat you abusively or unfairly.

Last month, I read in the news about a stranger who
bumped into LaQuedra Edwards while she was in a con-
venience store in the process of buying a lottery ticket at a
vending machine. The guy scooted off without a word—no,
"I'm sorry. Please excuse me." Because of the bump, she
accidently hit the wrong button and bought a $30 single
lottery ticket out of the vending machine rather than the
$40 ticket she had intended to buy, out of which she was
planning to select several options. She was irritated with the
guy, but there wasn't much she could do. Once she got to
her car, she scratched the card and realized she had won the
grand prize of $10 million dollars.[6]

Sometimes life works out that way. We get upset and
frustrated because someone opposes us or treats us unjustly
and we want to hold on to our right to be offended, but
there's so much we don't know. We don't know how God

6. See Sareen Habeshian, "Woman Wins $10M Lottery Jackpot after Accidentally
Pushing Wrong Button," Nexstar Media Wire, April 6, 2022, www.wkbn.com
/news/national-world/woman-wins-10m-lottery-jackpot-after-accidentally
-pushing-wrong-button.

will redeem our situations. It doesn't make the way we have been treated right, but it does mean we don't have to despair but rather that we can depend on God's grace to redeem and work things for our good. The difficulty may not produce something good in our lives as quickly as it did for LaQuedra, but good will come.

Jesus continues. "The time is coming when anyone who kills you will think they are offering a service to God" (John 16:2). The disciples were probably thinking, *Wait, didn't you mean to say, "Those who attempt to kill you"?—because it sure sounded like you just said that some of us will be killed.* Then Jesus says in verse 4, "I have told you this, so that when their time comes you will remember that I warned you about them."

Jesus says, in effect, "I'm telling you these things so you won't fall away. In those moments, you're going to remember that I warned you about this. You'll look at one another and say, "We knew this was gonna happen. What's the one thing Jesus told us to do when life isn't working the way we hoped it would: *stay connected*."

Sometimes people disconnect from Jesus because they begin to think that the waves they're encountering not only are God's fault; they also prove that he doesn't seem to care. I used to have a TikTok account.[7] I would justify it by saying I need to stay culturally relevant, but I kind of liked it a lot. Somehow my algorithm started showing me videos of kids getting hurt in humorous ways. Videos with the hashtag

---

7. I'm not proud of that, and it's possible I only deleted the app during the time I wrote this chapter so I could put that sentence in the past tense.

#kidsgettinghurt have more than 200 million total views. For some reason, there's a pretty big market for that type of video. I don't understand who would want to watch these videos. I don't see the appeal. It's insensitive. It's sad. It's laughing at someone else's pain. It's kinda funny. It's pretty hilarious. *I can't stop watching these videos.*

It's so easy for me to laugh at a kid falling off a slide and into a giant puddle or getting obliterated by a giant yoga ball because I don't know the child. There's nothing I can do to help them. I'm digitally detached from them. I'm sure their parents wouldn't have posted the video if the child had gotten badly hurt. So I enjoy the temporary misfortune of these little toddlers from afar. I think many people think God is like this—that he's scrolling through his heavenly TikTok app finding entertainment in our suffering from a distance.

Psalm 34:18 reveals and reminds us of God's character: "The Lord is close to the brokenhearted and saves those who are crushed in spirit." It's important to note that the presence of suffering in our lives does *not* indicate the lack of God's presence. Rather, the presence of suffering suggests that God is uniquely close and present. God wants the (sometimes) overwhelming waves of life to connect us more deeply with him as we discover his presence in ways we have never known before.

Holy Manure

Let's connect this back to our controlling metaphor from John 15 of "the vine and the branches." In agriculture, manure is an effective fertilizer that promotes health and growth. Manure may not smell pleasant, but it is used to bring forth greater fruitfulness.

When we find ourselves in the manure moments of life, our instinct is to get through them as quickly and painlessly as possible. Jesus tells his followers again and again to remain in him, but when we're surrounded by manure, the last thing we want to do is wait for the growth.

Becoming healthy fruit-bearing branches involves waiting while the manure does its work and trusting that the Gardener is allowing something unpleasant to cultivate growth. I'm sure I'm not the only one who gets impatient in the manure. When something difficult is happening, I want to fix it as quickly as possible. Apparently, I'm what you call a "flapper." At least that's what my ~~executive coach~~ therapist described to me.

Apparently, birds have about[8] three different ways of flying. One way of flying is gliding. Gliders will flap their wings and then just glide, but before long, they'll have to flap again. Other birds are soarers. Not very many birds can soar, but an eagle is one example. She will extend her powerful wings and catch the warm winds that blow over the earth. She will soar to great heights, reaching altitudes of more than ten thousand feet. She is not making flying happen by frantically flapping. Finally, there are flappers. When flappers flap, they defeat gravity by simply flapping

---

8. I say "about" just in case an ornithologist reads this book. Not to stereotype, but ornithologists can be sensitive.

fast enough. Some birds will flap those wings as much as a hundred times a second.

When things aren't going my way and the emotions of discouragement, frustration, anxiety, and even fatigue start flashing on the dashboard of my life, my instinct is to start violently flapping. Yet those moments provide an opportunity for me to deepen my connection with God. The prophet Isaiah put it this way, "Those who hope in the LORD will renew their strength. They will soar on wings like eagles" (40:31).

At the end of John 16, Jesus promises that trouble will come—and in John 17, trouble arrives. John 17 depicts a deeply intimate scene between Jesus the Son and God his Father. Jesus pours his heart out in prayer on behalf of his twelve disciples . . . and his disciples today. The request he makes to the Father in verses 15–17 can assist us as we attempt to shift our perspective on the waves of this world: "My prayer is not that you take them out of the world but that you protect them from the evil one. They are not of the world, even as I am not of it. Sanctify them by the truth; your word is truth."

Jesus doesn't pray that God will give them a trouble-free life. He could have asked him to scoop them up with all of their friends and family and transport them safely to some tropical paradise island where they could live out their lives comfortably. Instead, he prays for them to be protected against the plans of the enemy—that God will sanctify them.

Being sanctified is essentially becoming more and more

like Jesus. It's the removal of the corrupt parts of our souls and the addition of the Christlike character God wishes to develop in us. The very first command in the book of James is for believers to rejoice when they face a variety of trials, because God uses those trials to mature them (James 1:2–4). His message to the disciples and to us today is this: no matter what trouble descends on you, stay connected with the vine and trust that the Father will grow good fruit in your lives.

I often make reference to a fascinating psychological exercise I read about. John Ortberg suggests the following scenario:

> Imagine you have a child and you are handed a script of her entire life laid out before you. Better yet, you are given an eraser and five minutes to edit out whatever you want. . . . With this script of your child's life before you and five minutes to edit it, *what would you erase?* That is the question the psychologist Jonathan Haidt asked in this hypothetical exercise: *Wouldn't you want to take out all the stuff that would cause them pain?*[9]

Let's let this play out. You are reading your child's life story, their script. You learn that during elementary school, your daughter's learning disorder makes it difficult for her to thrive in school, to achieve what comes easily for every other kid. Erase it!

---

9. John Ortberg, *The Me I Want to Be: Becoming God's Best Version of Yourself* (Grand Rapids: Zondervan, 2010), 232.

Read a little bit further, and you find out that she wanted to play basketball in high school. But her class at school is full of extraordinarily talented athletes, which leads to her not making the final cut for the team. I'd erase that!

She goes off to college, starts dating a guy you don't feel good about from the beginning because he looks like the villain in every romantic comedy movie. Stereotypically, he cheats on her, breaks her heart, and sparks her downward spiral into a bout with depression that lasts two years. I'm erasing that heartbreak quicker than that punk ex-boyfriend can flip his hair.

She graduates from college and gets a job in a field she's passionate about. She's recovering some sense of purpose in her life. She calls you to tell her she thinks a promotion may be on the table. A week later, she calls you again and through tears informs you that instead of a promotion, her job position has been eliminated. You'd erase that too, wouldn't you?

It's just our natural instinct to erase difficulties from our lives and the lives of others around us because we think we're being protective. *But what if the pruning is the protection?* What if the pruning in some of the painful moments is protecting them in ways you can't perceive? What if that pruning is producing in them something they will desperately need later?

In my limited knowledge, I would have erased the learning disability that God used to produce perseverance and determination in my daughter. I would have erased the disappointment of her not making the team, but what if God is going to use that disappointment to root my daughter's sense of identity and value more securely in him? I would have erased the breakup or job loss that God would use to reveal to her the extent of his provision and care for her.

By erasing these losses and challenges, I would have protected her from the waves and pulled her out of the manure—and she would have missed the connection and character growth that God is producing in her life.

I know we're more comfortable with hypothetical exercises, but before moving on to the final chapter, I invite you to do something difficult. Take a few minutes to revisit the waves in your life. Maybe they dwell in the past, or maybe they're currently crashing around you. In your real life, name some of the difficult moments and how you are responding. I've been a pastor long enough to know that the waves don't necessarily cast people on the Rock of Ages; sometimes waves drag people out to sea. What waves are you experiencing, and how does God want to use those waves to connect more deeply with you and grow you?

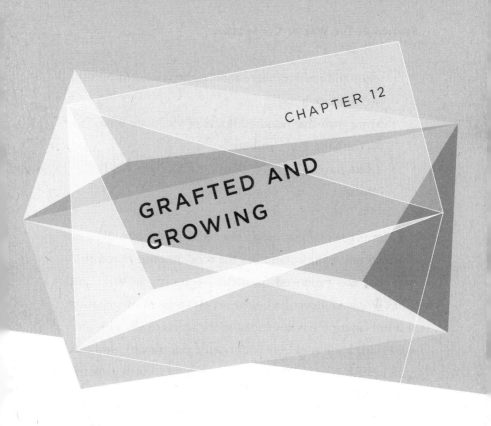

CHAPTER 12

GRAFTED AND GROWING

The phrase "information overload" is a phrase we hear a lot these days. We have exponentially more information available to us today than at any other time in history—it's not even close.

At the time of this writing, the average American is exposed to about 54,000 words and 443 minutes of video every day through time spent on social media and the internet.

- There are enough new tweets every day to write a ten-million-page book.
- The average person under the age of forty-five

sends and receives more than eighty-five text messages each day.

- More than five hundred hours of video are uploaded to YouTube every minute.
- There have been more than 2 trillion searches for information on Google per year.[1]

Here's the one that blows my mind: Every two days, we create as much information as the total amount of information that was produced from the beginning of time until 2003. We have never had more access to more information, and information has never had more access to us. The average smartphone user gets 63.5 notifications every day. And each notification alerts them to a piece of information that seems urgent.[2]

All of this information overload has led to a syndrome

---

1. For information on these statistics, see Casey Phillips, "Pullin the Plug: Facing Overload, Many Social Media Users Take a Vacation," *Chattanooga Times Free Press*, January 5, 2014, www.timesfreepress.com/news/2014/jan/05/breaking-ties; Athima Chansanchai, "Every Day the World Writes a '10 Million Page Book' in Tweets," NBC News: TechNews, July 1, 2011, www.nbcnews.com/tech/tech-news/every-day-world -writes-10-million-page-book-tweets-flna122444; "Worldwide Texting Statistics," Vermont State Highway Safety Office, https://shso.vermont.gov/sites/ghsp/files /documents/Worldwide%20Texting%20Statistics.pdf, accessed January 27, 2023; L. Ceci, "Hours of Video Uploaded to YouTube Every Minute 2007–2020," Statista, January 9, 2023, www.statista.com/statistics/259477/hours-of-video-uploaded-to -youtube-every-minute; Danny Sullivan, "Google Now Handles at Least 2 Trillion Searches per Year," Search Engine Land, May 24, 2016, https://searchengineland .com/google-now-handles-2-999-trillion-searches-per-year-250247; MG Siegler, "Eric Schmidt: Every 2 Days We Create as Much Information as We Did up to 2003," TechCrunch, August 4, 2010, https://techcrunch.com/2010/08/04/schmidt-data.
2. See Elle Hunt, "One Ping after Another: How Constant Notifications Are Driving Us Crazy," *Guardian*, January 27, 2020, www.theguardian.com/lifeandstyle/2020 /jan/27/one-ping-after-another-how-constant-notifications-are-driving-us-to -distraction.

called "IFS" (information fatigue syndrome). IFS has a number of side effects, but I want to draw your attention to two in particular:

1. **More external input means less internal reflection.** The more external input we receive, the less time and space we take for internal reflection. For example, let me ask you a question. It's kind of personal, so you don't need to answer it out loud, but here's my question: *Do you like who you are?* When is the last time you really stopped to reflect on that question? When is the last time you paused to ask yourself, *Do I like who I have become and am becoming?* All of our connection with what's happening *around* us has left us very little margin to connect with what's happening *in* us.

2. **It's increasingly difficult to prioritize what's important.** When the flow of information is continual and always feels urgent, everything is made to seem important. And if *everything* is important, then *nothing* is important. Our inability to prioritize information has left us feeling one of two extremes—either overwhelmed and stressed out, or apathetic and depressed.

In our information overload culture, we sometimes think that what we need is more information. When our way isn't working, we've been conditioned to Google our way out of it. We think that maybe there is some new information we haven't stumbled on. Maybe there's a new podcast that will fix whatever isn't working. We've tried to connect to the "information vine," thinking it will produce something different—that will give us the help and hope we need—but it doesn't.

Imitation Vines

Within all of us is the need to connect and the desire to produce. We instinctively want to feel connected, to know and be known. We intuitively want to produce and have something to show for our lives. From our childhood on, we're looking to be grafted into some kind of vine in which we can find acceptance and purpose. When Jesus introduces the vine and the branches metaphor to the disciples in John 15, he begins by saying in verse 1, "I am the true vine." The word *true*, also translated as "real," indicates the presence of other vines that aren't true or real. Imitation vines promise to give us the nutrients we need to produce and grow, but they don't.

The "information vine" is only one example of an imitation vine. Another popular fake vine is the "politics vine." People look around and feel frustrated, even enraged with the way things are in this world, and they desperately want things to be different. They think the political approach will produce something better. But there's a reason the kingdom that Jesus brought was not a democracy. He didn't run for president and turn his disciples into senators and representatives—though even at the time, it was the approach most people wanted Jesus to take. They wanted to make him king. But the politics vine doesn't work. It promises to produce change by means of power and to legislate a different kind of fruit. Like information, politics is important and certainly not irrelevant, but it's not the "true vine."

Another popular imitation vine is the "romance vine." You connect with that special someone, that soulmate, that main squeeze, that ride or die—and subconsciously, maybe even consciously, you think to yourself, *This person will be my true source of strength. This is the one who has been missing all my life. I know they will meet all my needs.* So you look them in the eye and say, "You're the meaning in my life; you're the inspiration." And before she realizes you're quoting Chicago's lyrics, you end it with a Jerry Maguire quote: "You complete me."

Your spouse was never meant to be your vine, and when you put that kind of pressure on them, things start to crack. You start to feel rejection, and there is nothing more devastating to your soul than feeling rejected by the person you've turned into a vine. When you connect with a significant other as your vine, you are essentially saying to them, "You be Jesus to me. I want you to do for me what only the Holy Spirit can do." That's a lot to ask, and eventually they'll start to resent it. And, of course, they can't possibly make it happen.

Another common imitation vine is the "me vine." Not *me* as in *me*. I'm not suggesting there's some *"Kyle vine"* that everyone is trying to connect to. But *me* as in *yourself.* After trying enough imitation vines, you recognize that none of them deliver the strength and nutrients you desperately need. You decide that you truly can only count on yourself. Maybe you become more obsessed with self-help and personal growth, or you focus in on exercise, nutrition, and self-care. Again, all of these things can be good, but if you put your hope in yourself, you will always be disappointed.

There are plenty of other imitation vines to be aware of. Maybe you've tried to connect to the imitation vine of success, wealth, entertainment, pleasure, or maybe even religion. All of them might promise you a fruit that will finally satisfy you, but it's not the kind of fruit that will last as Jesus describes in John 15.

Here's the thing about imitation vines: they can only bear imitation fruit.

Have you ever gone to someone's home and walked into the kitchen where you saw what appeared to be a delicious bowl of fruit? Maybe you even picked up a piece to eat, but before you could take a bite, you could tell by the weight and texture that it wasn't real. It looked real, real enough to create an appetite and hunger for it, but it was fake fruit. It could never deliver on what it promised.

Fake fruit promises to bring *authentic joy*, but it only brings *momentary pleasure*.

Fake fruit promises to bring *true purpose*, but it only brings *temporary distraction*.

Fake fruit promises to bring *real peace*, but it only brings a *brief diversion*, usually followed by deep emptiness.

Fake fruit promises to bring *genuine success*, but it only brings *shallow victory* and *passing admiration*.

Connecting with an imitation vine only brings imitation fruit.

Another Sad Stick Story

In my office I have a stick about three feet long that sits in the corner of the room. It's a stick I found on the ground behind my house. I don't know the story of that stick. I'm not sure what kind of tree it was once connected with. My guess is that the story of this stick on the ground involves a storm. Storms have a way of turning branches into sticks.

Joined to this stick are pieces of plastic fruit. I've tied the fake fruit to the stick with some wire. From a distance, it looks like a branch leaning against the wall and growing healthy fruit. When you get close enough to examine it, you can see it for what it is. It's not real. I keep it there to remind me of how I'm sometimes tempted to live my life. Instead of being a branch that is connected with the true vine, I settle for being a stick with some fake fruit attached to it. From a distance nobody seems to notice. As long as I don't let anyone get too close, I get away with it. But none of it is real, and as impressive as it might look from far away, all of it is worthless.

I heard an expression not long ago that I think reflects this dynamic: "do it for the gram." Even if you've never heard this clause, you might be able to guess what it means. It's the decision to do something for the sole purpose of taking a picture and posting it on Instagram. Imagine a couple goes out on a date, and even though they are feeling disconnected and are dealing with some genuine conflict, they are constantly posing and taking pictures so they can have something to post. It's not real, but it reinforces the way they want people to see them. Jesus warns about a "do it for the gram" approach to following him. Don't just go through the motions and pretend, he teaches us. In Matthew 23, Jesus warns the religious leaders who do things for others to see but whose hearts are far from him.

In John 15:6 (NLT), Jesus says, "Anyone who does not remain in me is thrown away like a useless branch and withers. Such branches are gathered into a pile to be burned." The Greek word here is translated as "branch," but what do you call a branch that isn't connected with a vine? You call it a *stick*. What do you do with sticks? You gather them and throw them into a fire. Or a wood chipper. Either way, it's not a happy ending.

One of my favorite news stories from 2020 had this headline: "Calif. Mom Crushed to Learn Plant She Watered for 2 Years Is Fake."[3] (My algorithm knows me so well. Of course I clicked on that.) Here's a quote in the story from Caelie Wilkes: "I was so proud of this plant. It was full, beautiful coloring, just an overall perfect plant. . . . I had a watering plan for it, if someone else tried to water my succulent I would get so defensive because I just wanted to keep good care of it. I absolutely loved my succulent."

---

3. Mike Moffitt, "Calif. Mom Crushed to Learn Plant She Watered for 2 Years Is Fake," SFGate, March 4, 2020, www.sfgate.com/bayarea/article/SAHM-mom -waters-fake-plant-succulent-15105213.php.

So how did she discover the truth? One day, she decided to transplant the succulent into a larger container and discovered the plant was plastic. Wilkes goes on to say, "I put so much love into this plant! I washed its leaves. Tried my hardest to keep it looking its best, and it's completely plastic! How did I not know this?"

Lots of questions. The first of which is why she ever told anyone about this story. If a news outlet questioned me about a plastic plant I had been watering for two years, I would respond with "no comment" and accusations of "fake news." The second question I have is this: How did she not know? If you're watering a plastic plant, where does the water go? I know I don't have to tell you this, but apparently succulents require very little water. She wasn't giving it much and simply thought the excess was just water that wasn't being soaked up. Wilkes has since replaced the plant with several real succulents. She threw away the fake one.

Imagine how foolish you would feel if you were to spend years caring for a fake plant because you thought it was real. Imagine spending years giving your time and energy to something that would never produce anything real.

Growing Real Fruit

When I try to make fruit grow out of an imitation vine, not only do I not produce real fruit, but I often also end up producing the opposite. Here's what I mean.

Let's say I look at the fruit of the Spirit and pick four

things from that list I need to grow in my life (Galatians 5:22–23). Perhaps I choose to focus on growing joy, peace, patience, and goodness. Jesus makes it clear that this fruit is produced by the Spirit when we are connected with him. But suppose I try to produce them on my own. Here what is likely to happen:

- If I try to produce *joy* in my life without being connected with the Vine, I end up feeling discouraged and sad because the harder I try, the more elusive it becomes. This is sometimes referred to as the "happiness paradox." The more you pursue happiness for its own sake, the more self-focused you become and the more out of reach it is.
- If I try to produce *peace* on my own, instead of serenity flowing from a connection with the Vine, I end up feeling stressed. It's incredibly stressful to keep telling yourself to have peace when it's not happening. It's like lying in bed and trying hard to fall asleep. That effort makes it that much harder to relax.
- If I try to grow in *patience* on my own, I will soon feel frustrated and impatient with my lack of progress. Now I'm not just impatient over my circumstances; I'm impatient over my impatience.
- If I try to grow in *goodness* without being connected with the Vine, whatever fruit I produce will likely end up rotten and ruined by ugly self-righteousness.

My oldest daughter's best friend in kindergarten was a girl named Jana Robey. I have many memories of looking in the rearview mirror and seeing those two girls giggling and being silly in the back seat. I never would have imagined that sixteen years later, I'd be standing in the front of a church sanctuary officiating Jana's funeral. For six and a half years, she had battled cancer with incredible courage and faith.

During that time, cancer took so much from her. She couldn't hear very well, was losing her sight, and spent much of her time in a wheelchair. Due to some paralysis in her face, she struggled to speak clearly. *Manure* isn't a strong enough word to describe what she had to deal with in this life. Cancer robbed Jana of being able to do much, but I was amazed at how much her life produced. Jana taught all of us what it looked like to stay connected and to abide in Christ when the waves just kept on coming.

Whenever I officiate a funeral, I sit down with close friends and family members who knew the person best and ask, "What was this person known for?" Sometimes the room is quiet and people aren't sure what to say. Sometimes the answers are profoundly sad. A mother once told me her twenty-eight-year-old son was known for his hat collection. An older widow once told me her husband was best known for his car collection. I found both answers equally depressing.

When I asked Jana's friends and family, "What was Jana known for?" I'm not sure what I was expecting them to say.

She didn't hold any records in sports activities. She didn't have any titles or advanced degrees. I started writing down the things that people told me about her life.

An older uncle, who was a pastor, said, "She transformed my prayer life."

An older aunt said, "She taught me to be grateful and to not complain."

A younger cousin said, "She taught me that faith in Jesus is really real."

Then I asked myself, *What words would you use to describe Jana?* Here's what I wrote down in my notes:

- **Peace.** She fought cancer for years and was constantly in and out of the hospital dealing with all kinds of pain and disappointment, but she was known for peace.
- **Kindness.** If anyone had a right to feel sorry for themselves and put their needs first, it was Jana, but she was known for her thoughtfulness toward others. She was the one who would regularly send prayer notes and cards of encouragement.
- **Faithfulness.** Even though it seemed that her prayers were never answered the way she wanted, Jana never turned away from God. She was faithful and testified of God's faithfulness to the end.
- **Love.** Jana was known for the way she loved people—not just the friends and family in that room that day, but the dozens of doctors and nurses who had cared for her over the years.

- **Joy.** That was actually the first word mentioned and the one most repeated. Six and a half years of pain and suffering—and she was known for joy? I remembered a year earlier when she was a guest on my podcast, she was sharing her story and I was trying to get her to complain about how hard things had been so the listeners would better understand what she had been through. She just wouldn't do it. I tried to prompt her: "Jana, what about losing your hair as a teen girl; that must have been difficult." Her response: "Yeah, it was, but I've always liked to wear hats."

Later that night, I pulled out my notebook and looked at the words I had written and felt chills run up and down my arms. There was something familiar about those words that I didn't notice when I was writing them down. Maybe you've already picked up on it. I started circling the words in the order they're found in Scripture: love, joy, peace, kindness, faithfulness. Without even meaning to, the people who knew her best used words from the list of the fruit of the Spirit in Galatians 5. She had stayed connected with Jesus. While spending so much time in the manure of this world, was it really a coincidence that this was the fruit her life produced?

Grafting Then Growing

As I studied the metaphor of vine and branches from John 15, I visited with a horticulturalist who helped me unpack some of the spiritual parallels. I learned about a process called "grafting." It's the process in which a gardener surgically connects a previously disconnected branch to a tree or to a plant of some sort. It's a beautiful image of what God has done for us through Jesus. When we try to bear meaningful and lasting fruit on our own, we are taking the "Caelie Wilkes approach" to life. We may be working hard and staying busy, but nothing is actually happening. No connection or production is really taking place. It's like picking up a stick and setting it in the corner and expecting it to produce something. We can water the stick and make sure it gets plenty of sunlight, but nothing is going to happen. Nothing is going to grow.

The only chance that a stick ever has of growing fruit is if the gardener grafts it into the vine.

The basic premise of this book is that when our way isn't working, the most important thing we can do is focus on our connection with the Vine. When your way isn't working and you feel discouraged, frustrated, anxious, or worn-out, just be the branch. The process of grafting reminds us that connection is always possible.

When a gardener connects a disconnected branch, he strips the branch clean of everything unhelpful—the twigs, the shoots, the leaves. All that remains is a stick. Then he takes that stick and connects it to the vine with a very particular technique. He cuts a wedge into the vine. He damages the vine so that the stick can be reconnected. Do you want to know what that technique is called?

It's called *bleeding*.

The gardener joins together the stick and the vine in that place where the vine has been cut, where it's bleeding. The vine bleeds, thereby making a way for a stick to become a branch. Over time the nutrients from the vine eventually move into the branch, causing it to bear fruit again.

Just in case you're not tracking with the metaphor, Jesus bled so that sticks could become branches, and branches could bear good fruit. As the true vine, Jesus makes a way for sticks that have fallen off, that seem to have no purpose, and no hope to become branches once again. Jesus' death on the cross is the one thing—the only thing—that makes connection possible.

In John 16, Jesus ends his Farewell Discourse by warning his followers, "In this world you will have trouble" (v. 33). But that's not the end of the verse (or the story). He follows up this warning with a promise to keep us connected: "Take heart! I have overcome the world." No matter what happens, even when things never seem to work out your way, be the branch and stay connected with the vine.

Go Deeper with the
Companion Video Study

Study Guide plus Streaming Video
9780310140528

DVD
9780310140542

Available now at your favorite bookstore,
or streaming video on StudyGateway.com.

Not a Fan

Becoming a Completely Committed Follower of Jesus

Updated and Expanded

Kyle Idleman

Not a Fan has already called more than one million readers to consider the demands and rewards of being a true disciple—moving from fan to follower in their relationship with Jesus.

After years of serving God, pastor and bestselling author Kyle Idleman had a startling revelation: for too long, he had been living as a fan of Jesus—someone who tried to make Christianity seem as appealing, comfortable, and convenient as he could to others. Idleman decided something had to change. He needed to embark on the journey of becoming a completely committed follower of God, not just a fan.

Fans want to be close enough to Jesus to get all the benefits but not so close that it requires sacrifice, while followers are all in and completely committed to Christ. *Not a Fan* gives you the tools you need to determine exactly where you stand when it comes to your relationship with Jesus.

No matter where you are in your walk with Christ, *Not a Fan* calls you to consider the demands and rewards of being a true disciple. With frankness and a touch of humor, Idleman invites you to:

- Examine your relationship with God
- Determine if you're following Jesus or just following the rules
- Pray the way Jesus prayed
- Start truly living for the One who gave his all for you

This expanded and updated version includes a new introduction and an entirely new chapter about how to live out the book's core message.

Join Idleman as he challenges you to take an honest look at your relationship with Jesus, and discover what it really means to be a follower.

Available in stores and online!

ZONDERVAN®
.com

Not a Fan Daily Devotional

75 Days to Becoming a Completely Committed Follower of Jesus

Kyle Idleman

Your day-by-day guide to living out the message of the mega-bestseller *Not a Fan*. Perfect for those looking to take the next steps in being a disciple of Jesus.

Not a Fan calls you to consider the demands and rewards of being a true disciple. With frankness sprinkled with humor, Pastor Kyle Idleman invites you to live the way Jesus lived, love the way he loved, pray the way he prayed, and never give up living for the One who gave his all for you.

This devotional offers seventy-five days of insights, stories, encouragement, and biblical truth and inspiration. Each devotional gives a Scripture to focus on, a story or insight that illustrates one of the *Not a Fan* principles, and, most importantly, a "Do Something about It" section that suggests simple ways to put the principles into practice immediately.

Also available: *Not a Fan* Spanish edition, journal, student and teen editions, small group study, and more.

Available in stores and online!

Gods at War

Defeating the Idols that Battle for Your Heart

Kyle Idleman

Join pastor and bestselling author Kyle Idleman as he illustrates a clear path away from the heartache of our twenty-first-century idolatry and back to the heart of God, enabling us to be completely committed followers of Jesus.

What do Netflix, our desire for the corner office, and that perfect picture we just posted on Instagram have to do with each other? None of these things are wrong in and of themselves. But when we begin to allow entertainment, success, or social media to control us, we miss out on the joy of God's rule in our hearts.

In *Gods at War*, Idleman helps every believer recognize that there are false gods at war within each of us, and they battle for the place of glory and control in our lives.

According to Idleman, idolatry isn't *an* issue; it is *the* issue. And he reveals which false gods we are allowing on the throne of our lives by asking such insightful questions as:

- What do you sacrifice for?
- What makes you mad?
- What do you worry about?
- Whose applause do you long for?

We're all wired for worship, but we often end up honoring the idols of money, sex, food, romance, success, and many others that keep us from an intimate relationship with God.

In this updated and expanded edition, Idleman adds a new introduction and new content about the battle many of us face with technology—whether we are tempted to send just one more text, stay online when our bodies need rest, or put email before in-person relationships—teaching us how to seek God with our whole heart.

Available in stores and online!